Understanding
TREES

Understanding
TREES

A Guide to Tree Health and Selection
in the Central Valley of California

John K. Pape

Craven Street Books
Fresno, California

UNDERSTANDING TREES
A Guide to Tree Health and Selection
in the Central Valley of California
By John K. Pape

Text and photos, except as noted, © John Pape 2006
Drawings © Linden Publishing 2006

135798642

Cover art by James Goold
Book design by Carla Green

ISBN 10: 1-933502-05-3
ISBN 13: 978-1-933502-05-2
Printed in Thailand

Pape, John K.
    Understanding trees : a guide to tree health and selection in the
Central Valley of California / by John K. Pape.
        p. cm.
    "A Craven Street book."
    Includes index.
    ISBN-13: 978-1-933502-05-2 (pbk. : alk. paper)
    ISBN-10: 1-933502-05-3 (pbk. : alk. paper)
    1. Trees, Care of—California—Central Valley. I. Title.
    SB435.52.C22P37 2006
    635.9'77097945--dc22   2006022660

A Craven Street Book
Linden Publishing Inc.
2006 S. Mary, Fresno CA
www.lindenpub.com
800-345-4447

I dedicate this book to Ken and Zelma Pape, my parents.
I was beyond lucky.

CONTENTS

ACKNOWLEDGEMENTS

Thanks to God for the time on this beautiful planet, with its trees, and His grace.

Thanks to Lori, Renae and Evan for their expression of love in letting me steal from their time for this book.

Thanks to Richard Sorsky for giving me a chance to publish.

Thanks to all my friends in the green industry for helping me to learn.

PREFACE

The purpose of this book is to help you enjoy, and extend the life of, some of the most valuable items you own, your trees. Except for your home, trees are frequently of more value than any of your other material possessions. They are often more valuable than your automobile. Nowadays you can hire a Certified Arborist to place a value on your trees and that value could range from $100 to $20,000 each.

The purpose of this book is to inform you, without being too technical, of some fascinating, and critical, facts and concepts about trees. More importantly, it will show you how knowing that information can enhance your experience with trees as well as your property value.

It is easy to see that most people who develop, sell, or manage, real estate understand the value of trees (although you can see that some don't have a clue). Developers, especially of shopping centers and other commercial sites, spend hundreds of thousands to millions of dollars on trees. Cities require developers to line streets with trees, plant trees in common areas, and plant trees in parking lots to create a pre-specified amount of shade. Folks who sell and lease real estate are constantly trying to increase the "curb appeal" of the locations they handle. This, to a great degree, requires appropriate, aesthetically pleasing, trees.

The Journal of Arboriculture, Volume 29, No. 5, September 2003

Fig. 1: An impressive quantity of trees are planted in our cities and suburbs.

reveals that trees and quality land-scaping around commercial build-ings does indeed increase the rental rates. In the article, *The Influence of Trees and Landscaping on Rental Rates at Office Buildings*, research shows that owners could gain an advantage of about seven percent in increased rental rates if their properties were planted with

Fig. 2: Parking spots under shady trees are always at a premium.

shading trees in an aesthetically pleasing landscape. Other reports have shown an increase in the sale price of residential properties of about four to seven percent, when good tree planting was a part of the landscape.

We usually take trees for granted. (Fig. 1) There are great numbers of them, many kinds, and they are all around us, so we typically overlook them, except of course when picking a parking spot or picnic table in the summer. (Fig. 2) Sometimes people will choose a new home because of the trees. Many times I have heard people say that great trees were the clincher in the purchase of their new home. "We bought this house because of the trees" is what they frequently say.

When we do stop to think about and appreciate trees we realize that they have had great significance throughout history and in our various religions. Have you ever heard of the Tree of Life, the Tree of the Knowledge of Good and Evil, Buddha's Bodhi Tree, or the Cedars of Lebanon? Trees are the largest living things, both in mass and height. They are among the oldest living things. Many people live in homes built to a great extent out of trees. This book and nearly every paper item you've ever read or touched comes from trees. I know you have already heard most of this information, but I'm trying to renew a sense of interest and appreciation, if not awe, for our silent, sturdy friends. (Fig. 3)

Trees play an important role in our environment. They filter great amounts of carbon out of the atmosphere. They help keep soil from eroding, increase water retention and mitigate some air pollution and heat island effect in cities. Heat island effect is the name given to the area of heat that builds up in and around our urban centers. The heat is generated by the sun, and our concentrated human activity, then absorbed and retained at a higher level for longer periods of time than in rural areas. This is mainly due to the materials we construct our cities out of, like concrete, asphalt, steel and glass. Trees, by providing shade to urban surfaces can help to minimize this effect. (Fig. 4, 5, 6)

"Planting trees in energy-conserving locations around buildings reduces carbon emissions from fossil-fuel-based power plants that more than compensates for maintenance carbon emissions. Trees in energy-con-

Fig. 3: In the Redwoods.

Susan Neri

serving locations lead to an annual net benefit of carbon reduction with a cumulative impact that increases through time. In addition, trees in non-energy-conserving sites also can have an overall impact on reducing urban carbon emissions by reducing air temperatures and consequent emissions associated with urban heat islands." — Journal of Arboriculture, Volume 28, No. 3, May 2002, *Effects of Urban Tree Management and Species Selection on Atmospheric Carbon Dioxide*

"Trees can capture significant quantities of health-damaging particles from the atmosphere with the potential to improve local air quality. There are marked species differences in the ability of trees to capture pollutant particles, such that conifers may be the best choice for pollution-control plantings. Among the broad-leaved species studied, those with rough leaf surfaces are most effective at capturing particles." — Journal of Arboriculture, Volume 26, No. 1, January 2000, *Effective Tree Species For Local Air-Quality Management.*

One of the most amazing facts about trees is that people

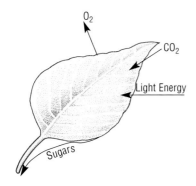

Fig. 4: Carbon removed from the air in the form of CO_2 combines with hydrogen and oxygen to create sugars by use of light energy. The carbon then becomes wood, root, leaf and flower and is stored until tree parts decay.

Roots slow and trap water and sediment, reducing erosion.

Fig. 5: Soil erosion reduction

who are physically or mentally ill get well faster if they are able to look out on green, park-like, well-treed areas. Roger S. Ulrich did a study over twenty years ago that showed a difference in the recovery rates of people who looked out their hospital window at a stand of trees versus those who looked out their window at a brick wall. Those patients viewing the trees needed less time to recover, required less and weaker drugs and were less negative. Since then more studies have been done showing that providing care to people in a more pleasant environment aids in their recovery. This applies to both physical and mental illness.

The vast number of tree species and the great variety of individual characteristics, sometimes makes it difficult to choose the correct tree for any specific use. Problems often arise because of the poor choice of tree for a location or conversely, the choice of location for a specific tree. Learn as much as you can about the trees you may choose and always try to find some of those species in a mature state so you can see exactly what you're going to have in the future.

Trees grow, we grow. Like any creature, trees can be injured or sick. Trees heal, we heal. The difference is trees do everything slowly. Unless extremely damaged, they don't show illness or the result of damage quickly, nor do they return to health quickly. Often when we first notice a problem with a tree, it has been a problem for some time. It may even be too late to remedy the situation. Because of this, it is

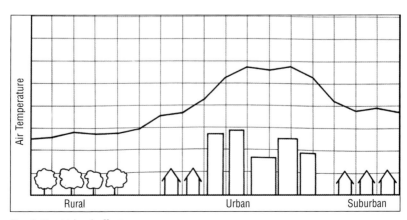

Fig. 6: Heat island effect

important to know what to look for and to look for it regularly. In this way you can help stop a serious problem with your tree before it goes too far. If in doubt, call out a tree doctor, an arborist, or horticulturist.

No specific pest control application methods are laid out in this book, only general guidelines. Always try to use a non-toxic or low-toxicity method of pest control first. When choosing a pesticide, even a low toxicity one, you must always find the pesticide that specifies your host plant on the label as well as the target pest you are attempting to kill or control. You must completely read the label of any pesticide before making an application. I suggest you read a label at least three times before applying any compound. I do. If you are not sure of what to do regarding pest control applications, call a professional, licensed, applicator. They have taken tests to verify their knowledge and are required to complete continuing education to keep up with the latest information. Typically, there are not many individuals well educated in tree pests and willing to do tree related pest control. You should attempt to find a "tree doctor" who is either a pest control applicator with knowledge of trees or an arborist with a license for pest control. Most large towns should have at least one company or individual that qualifies. Many effective spray or injection techniques for trees take specialized equipment that most of us don't have around the house.

Remember, except for the house itself, your trees are the largest and longest-term investment on your property, and they are worth a little professional help. If your dog or cat were very sick, you would likely take them to the veterinarian at least once, wouldn't you? The same idea should apply to a quality tree in your landscape.

> *Trees are living, growing, natural wonders that offer us an opportunity to link our daily lives with nature. In concrete and asphalt environments, trees are a powerful way to satisfy basic needs for a healthy human spirit. We should utilize and maximize these natural wonders to make our cities and suburbs livable and fulfilling.*
>
> — John M. Valentino

QUICK DIAGNOSIS TOOL

This section of the book is designed to help you quickly move to the chapter of the book that will be of the most assistance when you have an immediate problem. The following areas of concern are the most obvious and most basic, and are intended to lead you to a more thorough discussion of the possible problems and their solutions. The topics below are by no means a full description of the problems that a tree can have. Trees are complex organisms, frequently plagued by more than one problem at a time, but this is a good place to start.

Sticky tree?

If you notice nearly clear, sticky residue beneath a tree, or black mold covering the leaves of a tree and/or what is underneath it, you most likely have some sort of sucking insect such as aphids, scale, psyllids, or leafhoppers on the leaves or small branches of the tree. For more information regarding this problem see Chapter 5.

Holes in your leaves?

If your tree's leaves have irregularly shaped holes in them, especially at the edges and not in any regular pattern, you probably have a

Fig. 1: Obvious munching by chewing insects, probably caterpillars on a Butterfly Bush.

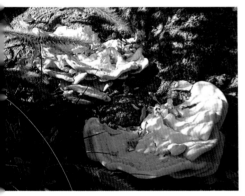

Fig. 2: Wood decay conks can be beautiful, but quite often problematic for a tree.

Fig. 3: Flathead borers destroying a tree. If you find these under the bark of your tree, you have serious trouble.

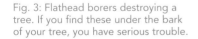

Fig. 4: The wavy line of holes indicates a sapsucker bird problem.

chewing type of insect, such as a grasshopper or caterpillar. For more information regarding this problem see Chapter 5. (Fig. 1)

Mushrooms growing from your tree?

If you notice a large, unusual mushroom-like growth protruding out of the side of the trunk of your tree or from a wound in the tree, you probably have a form of wood decay fungus living in the tree. For more information regarding this problem see Chapter 3. (Fig. 2)

Holes in your tree's trunk?

If you have small holes in the trunk and larger branches of your tree, you may have borers. The holes may have sap, or saw dust, or nothing coming out of them. If the holes appear to be nearly in a line circling the branch or trunk this is likely to be woodpecker damage, which is much less of a problem, but still can be destructive. For more information on these problems see Chapter 4. (Fig. 3, 4, 5)

Wilted leaves?

This is a difficult problem because it may be caused by too little water, too much water, or root disease. To find out what could be happening in the root zone of your tree see Chapter 1. (Fig. 6)

Dieback on the outside of your tree's canopy?

When there is more than a small amount of branch dieback on the outside of the canopy of the tree, there may be a serious problem. Inhospitable environmental conditions, root diseases, and branch diseases can be the cause. For more information on this problem see Chapter 4. (Fig. 7)

Fig. 6: It is obvious that there is a problem, but you may have to investigate carefully to find it.

Fig. 7: If you see this it is past time to search out the cause.

Fig. 5: A tree with this much damage by a carpenter worm is a doomed.

Fig. 8: If you see this, rest easy, it is a normal part of growth in a tree.

Fig. 9: If your plant is not supposed to be variegated, this color could mean trouble of several kinds.

Dieback on the inside of your tree's canopy?

This is usually not a problem, just a natural part of a trees growth and renewal on the outer part of the canopy. As it grows it jettisons older branches shaded in the interior. But, just to make sure, take a look at Chapter 4. (Fig. 8)

Yellowing leaves?

Yellowing leaves can be the result of a natural process of renewal in the tree as it jettisons old leaves, or it can be a sign of nutrient deficiency or root disease. For more information on the possibility of a deficiency or root disease see Chapter 1. (Fig 9)

Does your Modesto Ash or Sycamore have deformed leaves with brown blotches that fall off in the spring?

Your tree may have a very common leaf fungus disease called anthracnose that won't kill it, but can cause it stress, especially if the spring time is rainy. To find out more about this problem see Chapter 5. (Fig. 10)

Fig. 10: This is a common disease and can be treated if you choose.

Branches falling for no apparent reason?

Your tree may be suffering from a mysterious ailment particular to only certain trees. It is commonly called summer limb drop, or spontaneous limb drop. To find out more see Chapter 6.

Is your tree barely growing, and looks weak and discolored?

Maybe the bark has been damaged by sunscald or a string trimmer. These are extremely common problems, occurring more frequently than disease problems. To find out more see Chapters 2 and 3. (Fig. 11A, 11B, 11C, 12)

Fig. 11A: This tree is full of insects and decay due to years of sunscald.

Fig. 12: In cities and suburbs, more trees are damaged or killed by string trimmer damage than many other tree-killing problems combined.

Fig. 11B and 11C: More examples of decay due to sunscald.

Fig. 13: A common yet treatable disease.

Does your Flowering Pear tree have what looks like burnt foliage?

It is very likely that fire blight is the culprit. It is a bacterial disease that attacks pears and related trees. To find out more see Chapter 5 under Bacterial Leaf disease. (Fig. 13)

*What did the tree learn
from the earth to be able
to talk with the sky?*

—Pablo Neruda

CHAPTER 1

THE ROOTS

It's a dirty job, but somebody has to do it

Most people understand that the roots are pulling up water and mining nutrients from the soil, but roots do far more than most of us think about and in ways we do not realize. Roots not only send raw materials up to the canopy of the tree, but also anchor it solidly in the ground, store surplus carbohydrates and interact with soil microorganisms to benefit the tree. Most people envision the roots of a tree going very deep, thinking of the idea of a taproot and a root structure shaped and sized like the top of the tree. The truth is the root structure below the ground looks nothing in shape or size like the tree looks above ground. Usually the majority of roots exist only two to three feet below the surface and spread much wider than the canopy. (Fig. 1-1) There are exceptions. Some trees, like the Coastal Redwood (*Sequoia sempervirens*), a very popular tree in the Central Valley, add more and more fibrous roots to the same basic area. The roots do not spread very far, relative to trees like oaks or eucalyptus. This means that redwoods need more water placed on the same basic area of soil as they mature. The way roots match the top of the tree is in how much work they do. There is a balance, a reciprocity, between the work the canopy does and the work the roots do and how they supply each other's needs. Very much like a good marriage.

Fig. 1-1: Shape of top of tree vs. shape of roots

AERATION

What's really going on?

Although roots are vegetative, they are similar in some ways to humans and other animals. Roots, like animals, respire oxygen. A sort of fuel burning, or oxidation, takes place in roots. Oxygen consumption is critical to healthy roots. Oxygen can not easily penetrate more than the first few feet of soil and this limits the growth of a tree's root system.

Why it matters:

If a tree's roots do not receive substantial oxygen they cease to grow and do their work. They quit absorbing water and raw materials. That is one of the ironies of gardening. A plant with too much water will still wilt and die as if dry. Often times people will add more water at this point because of the wilted look. The water has pushed out all of the air from between the soil particles. Picture a jar full of one-inch stones. They will have spaces between them, which contain air. Then, picture filling the jar up with water. Out goes the air. Now imagine if you could open a small valve at the bottom of the jar. As the water flows out, air moves back in, although there would still be some moisture clinging to the stones.

This is exactly what happens in between the super fine soil particles a tree grows in. When roots stop picking up nutrients, leaves can become chlorotic (yellow) or brown, or fall off altogether. Trees in this situation are also much less resistant to disease.

Hard, compacted, soils frequently impair gas exchange between the surface and the roots below. Paving, like concrete and asphalt, which is impermeable to substantial gas exchange, can also cause much damage to existing trees if placed above their root zone.

What you can do:

You can apply slow, deep water to your trees leaving some time between watering for the soil to nearly dry out.

You can install aeration tubes. Typically, these tubes only need to go one foot to eighteen inches deep. The tubing needs to be perforated. These items, pre-made, can be purchased at informed nurseries or online. You can also make them out of either rigid or flexible drain line with perforations. The most common size used is three inches in diameter, and once installed, is frequently filled with pea gravel. (Fig. 1-2) These devices allow air to exchange with the soil somewhat faster and to a deeper level.

If you must install paving above the root zone of a tree, you can install a special aeration device to mitigate the effects of that paving. Before paving, create horizontal trenches to the depth of ten or twelve inches stretching radially out from the tree. (Fig. 1-3, 1-4) In the trenches, lay perforated drain line with at least one end turning up to open out into the air above the soil surface. The paving could then be placed over the covered trenches, leaving only the open end of the aeration device exposed in a planter somewhere near the tree.

Sometimes applications of soil amendments can aid in air penetration. Gypsum is often used for this purpose. Because the calcium ions in gypsum are more of a perfect match for the charge of soil particles, the particles will let go of other ions like sodium, and latch on to the calcium. The physical effect results in a slightly more open soil. Adding organic matter like compost, rice hulls, and wood fines, to the soil can also aid in keeping soils from becoming compacted. Other products such as John & Bob's Soil Optimizer, and yucca extract can be of use in opening up your soil.

Sometimes, to aid drainage, you can drill a very deep hole, backfill up to two feet from the surface with $1\frac{1}{2}$-inch crushed rock. Cover that with a permeable

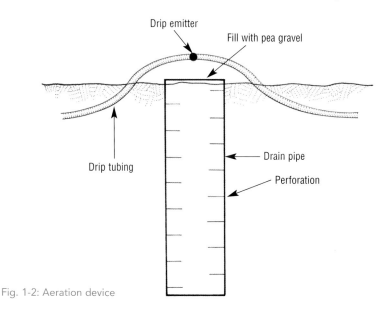

Fig. 1-2: Aeration device

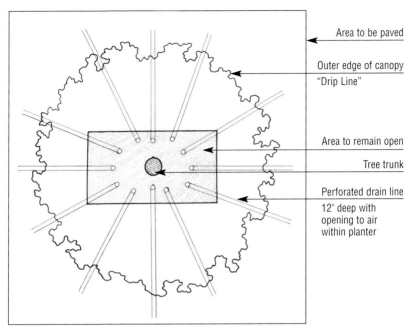

Area to be paved

Outer edge of canopy "Drip Line"

Area to remain open

Tree trunk

Perforated drain line
12" deep with
opening to air
within planter

Fig. 1-3: Trenching pattern for aeration under tree being paved around

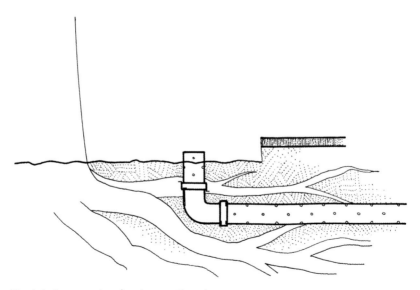

Fig. 1-4: Cross-section showing aeration pipe

landscape fabric, and then place good soil over the last one foot. This will allow excess water to penetrate through hardpan or difficult soil profiles. (Fig. 1-5)

THE RHIZOSPHERE
What's really going on?

The root zone (rhizosphere) is one of the most life-filled areas of our world. In addition to vertebrate and invertebrate organisms, there are an incredible variety of microorganisms living in the soil. For now, let's talk about the microorganisms. They arc extremely important to the life and health of trees. In the soil are fungi and bacteria that have intimate and sometimes exclusive relationships with various species of plants. There is a very complicated and only partially understood web of interactions between these microorganisms.

When trees create carbohydrates in the leaves, a certain amount is sent down to the roots as food. A small amount of these carbohydrates leak out of the roots. Many microorganisms, particularly some fungi, use this exudate as part, or all, of their nutrient supply. Some of the fungi are

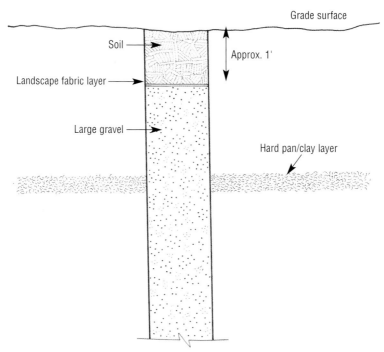

Fig. 1-5: Drainage hole using fabric

beneficial and some of them can be pathogenic (disease causing).

Why it matters:

The beneficial fungi have a symbiotic relationship with the roots. The fungus eats its meal of exudates and its mycelium (mat of root-like structures) act as a super fine extension of the tree's roots. This, in effect, increases the surface area penetrated by the tree's roots, and it increases the ability of the tree to gather nutrients, even from poor soils. These beneficial microorganisms can reduce the ability of pathogens (bad guys) to attack the roots by taking up space and resources along the root surface, not leaving any for the pathogens. You might imagine them as a bunch of big pigs keeping little pigs from getting to the food trough.

Pathogens will attack roots if they become abundant enough to overpower a tree's resistance, or if there is a weakness in the tree's defenses, or both. Sometimes the pathogens will destroy the tissues of the roots themselves and sometimes they will travel up into the vascular system of the tree, compromising its ability to move nutrients and water to the canopy. Ultimately, this can kill the tree. Some beneficial fungi can also attack some pathogens. Trichoderma fungus is one of these. Trichoderma is sold under brand names such as Plant Helper and Root Shield. It is an aggressive fungus, which takes up space and nutrients, out-competing malicious fungi, and sometimes even attacking them.

What you can do about it:

You can encourage beneficial microorganisms by applying good compost and compost tea on and in your soil. Some products like the organic John & Bob's Soil Optimizer contain soluble humus that helps to activate beneficial soil microorganisms.

Appropriate organic mulch, like bark, chips, and leaves can make the soil more hospitable to good fungi.

You can also inoculate your soil with beneficial fungi such as Trichoderma species or Mycorrhiza species. This would help to keep the pathogenic fungi down in numbers and strength, thus giving your tree some underground protection. In addition, some beneficial fungi actually enhance the tree's ability to mine water and raw materials from the soil. Beneficial fungi are becoming more available from informed nurseries and online.

FERTILIZATION

What's really going on?

Plants require a multitude of nutrients. The nutrients needed in the largest amounts are nitrogen, phosphorous and potassium. There are many other nutrients required in smaller quantities. These include calcium, sulfur, iron, zinc, manganese, magnesium, and copper. These less required nutrients are referred to as micronutrients. Nitrogen is the one nutrient that needs to be replaced in the soil in the largest amount, and most frequently. Two forms of nitrogen are taken up by plant roots, ammonium (NH_4) and nitrate (NO_3).

Why it matters:

The proper balance of ammonium and nitrate in the soil is important for a good balance of root growth,

Fig. 1-6: Take note of the lack of green tissue between the veins of the leaf.

shoot growth, and disease and insect resistance. High levels of immediate-release nitrogen fertilizers can put the two forms out of balance.

Although micronutrients are only needed in the smallest amounts, they are crucial to many plant processes. For example, when a plant does not have enough magnesium, the atom at the heart of the chlorophyll molecule, it will lose its green color and be unable to create its food. If a tree does not receive enough iron, used in one of the phases of photosynthesis, its leaves will become chlorotic (yellow, in this case between the veins) (Fig. 1-6), and eventually the tree can die. A lack of other micronutrients causes similar problems.

What you can do:

The primary way to avoid having an imbalance of nitrogen types is to fertilize with a slow-release fertilizer. This type of fertilizer releases the nitrogen component over a period of six months to a year.

If you need to make micronutrients available to your tree you can buy fertilizers that contain micronutrients. Sometimes if the pH level of the soil is too high the micronutrients in the soil will not be available to the tree's roots although they exist in the soil. In this case, you would want to acidify your soil by adding soil sulfur, peat moss, or other organic matter.

SURFACE ROOTS

What's really going on?

Many factors affect the degree to which you may get surface roots. Such factors include whether or not the tree is grown in turf, whether the soil is well drained, or how deeply air can penetrate into the soil. Some trees are genetically prone to have aggressive surface roots. They will likely have bad surface root problems no matter what circumstances they find themselves in.

Why it matters:

The main problem caused by surface roots is the destruction of sidewalks, driveways, fences and foundations. Surface roots can also cause tripping hazards. (Fig. 1-7) They create competition for raw materials and water with turf and other shallow-rooted plants. They are unattractive and, by being on the surface, can be easily damaged, thus exposing the tree to disease.

What you can do:

The most important thing you can do is to be careful and thoughtful when choosing a tree to plant. The best way to do that is to examine the same species of tree you are

Fig. 1-7: Surface roots like these are a common problem with certain species of trees.

considering in a mature form to see what it will become — gentle friend or aggressive monster.

Increasing air and water penetration is an important way to encourage deeper roots. Installing aeration devices and applying certain soil amendments (see Aeration, above) can do this.

Installation of root barriers is also an option. They are often made from semi-rigid plastic sheets, but can be made from thick rubber, steel, concrete or anything else that greatly reduces the ability of water or gases to pass through and resists penetration by the roots themselves. There is also a barrier made from fabric impregnated with a herbicide that inhibits cell division at the tips of the roots. These barriers should be installed to the depth of eighteen to thirty-six inches. Supply houses that cater to landscape contractors will have these barriers available. You may also want to check on-line.

If the roots have already caused a problem, you can dig them up and prune them. This is usually done with an axe. The cleaner the cut, the better. Ragged ends produced by trenching and similar equipment are not desirable. Any cut is an opening that diseases can use to penetrate the system of the plant, so this is not the first choice of action, but is often necessary. A barrier is usually added after this root pruning. Root pruning is best done in cool weather when the water demand on the tree is low. If you examine the ground around your young trees each winter as they grow, you can often spot small roots on, or just under the surface, before they become much bigger than your thumb. This is the time to easily prune them out before they become a problem. I frequently tell people to put this activity on their calendar once a year, similar to the way you would schedule cleaning out your gutters before the rainy season.

Except during the nine months before he draws his first breath, no man manages his affairs as well as a tree does.

— George Bernard Shaw

CHAPTER 2

THE ROOT CROWN
Getting to the Bottom of the Situation

The root crown is the area where the two most significant parts of a tree meet. Where the roots meet the trunk, often referred to as the base, is one of the most critical yet overlooked areas of a tree's anatomy. In some ways roots are like humans and other animals. They cannot make their own food. They must get it from the green parts of plants. From one point of view, you and I, and all non-photosynthesizing creatures, could be considered parasites of the green plants of this world. Roots, like animals, also store and breakdown carbohydrates. We store them mainly in the form of fat. Trees store them mainly in the form of starches. Much of the carbohydrates a tree stores are in the roots. The root crown is similar to a port of entry between two countries. All raw materials and water must travel across this area, and so must much of the carbohydrates that are either used by, or stored in, the roots. It is a crucial area where the character of the tree changes from carbon dioxide breathing and carbohydrate creating, to oxygen breathing and carbohydrate using. Damage to this part of a tree is potentially more dangerous than anywhere else. (Fig. 2-1)

CROWN ROT
What's really going on?
The bark on the roots of a tree is designed to function in the soil and has a natural resistance to infections from soil borne microorganisms. The bark on the trunk of a tree is usually not made

to defend itself from those microorganisms. It is designed to resist other microorganisms, insects, heat, wind, birds, and other threats commonly found above ground. There are many microorganisms living in the soil whose job it is to break down dead organic material. That is why if you leave anything organic on or in the soil long enough, under normal conditions, it will decay. The bark of a tree's trunk

Fig. 2-2: This type of mulching around trees is asking for trouble.

is dead inactive organic matter. It serves the tree as shield and barrier. The active part of the bark is the inner bark.

Why it matters:

A tree's outer bark, if exposed to saprophytic soil microorganisms long enough (the kind that break down dead, inactive organic matter), will succumb to those microorganisms, and be eaten through. (Fig. 2-2) This creates an opening for pathogens, usually fungi, to enter into and infect the active tissues of the tree. This process is much like a person getting an infection through a wound. These kinds of diseases in trees usually destroy the inner bark (phloem), the living, actively growing part of the trunk (cambium), and sometimes the active outer wood (xylem) part of the vascular system. This can be severely debilitating or fatal to a tree. (Fig. 2-3, 2-4) Even if an aggressive disease does

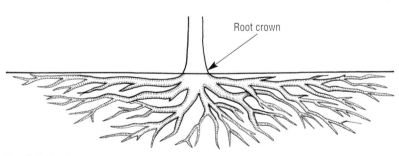

Root crown

Fig. 2-1: Root crown

not enter through the wound, a wood decay fungus could enter and begin the process of breaking down the deeper wood of the tree. These fungi slowly remove the lignin, cellulose, or both, from the cell walls of the wood tissue, turning the once sturdy wood to mush. This weakens the structural integrity of the tree and makes it more likely to fail, break or fall down. (Fig. 2-5, 2-6)

What you can do about it:
The number one point to remember is to never plant new woody shrubs or trees too deep. Many people drill deep holes where a tree is going to be planted to soften the soil for root penetration and for drainage. This is a fine idea, but can have a negative side effect. If you plant a tree in the softened soil from drilling, it can sink. After it sinks, over time, soil washes up against the trunk exposing the bark to damage by soil borne microorganisms. Flooding or tamping or both should repack the soil in a planting hole. Some people will plant the tree on a soil shelf created at the appropriate height on the side

Fig. 2-3: Note the dark stains caused by oozing from the diseased areas.

Fig. 2-4: The symptoms of crown rot can be subtle.

Fig. 2-5: These conks (fungal fruiting bodies) indicate weakness deep in the tree.

Fig. 2-6: The brown powder in this photo are spores that will blow in the wind to infect other trees.

of a drilled hole, or leave a pedestal of harder soil in the center of a hand dug hole. (Fig. 2-7) Trees should usually be planted with the top of the root ball about a half-inch above the level of the surrounding soil. Even in the most ideal situations the soil below the tree tends to compact, and even if it doesn't, it's better to have the root crown high than to have it too low.

Never install sprinklers in such a way as to have them spray directly onto the trunk of a tree.

This will almost certainly insure a future case of root crown rot. In general, it's better to have sprinklers apply water at least a foot or more away from the root crown, and out toward the edge of the drip line. There is one exception. It is advisable to place water at the edge of the root ball of a newly planted tree, even if this is fairly close to the trunk. This will get water to the existing roots and to the soil surrounding them, encouraging further growth. (Fig. 2-8) Once the tree has been estab-

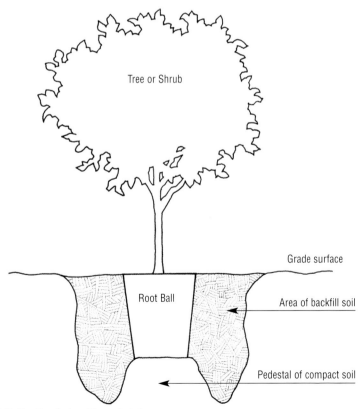

Tree or Shrub

Grade surface

Root Ball

Area of backfill soil

Pedestal of compact soil

Fig. 2-7: Planting hole with pedestal

lished, in a season or two, water should no longer be applied close to the trunk.

It is a good idea to make sure that moist organic matter, like mulch, leaves, humus, turf, or deep ground cover, is not left up against the root crown. This makes the susceptible bark available to saprophytic microorganisms. A bare area of soil 6 inches to 3 feet in radius around the base of a tree is usually the best situation.

If your tree is infected with root crown rot, and is not too far-

gone, it can be treated by injection with a fungicide labeled for that application. A professional should do this job. Because the disease attacks the vascular and surrounding tissues, the fungicide won't kill all of the disease, but it can stop the disease at its leading edge. This holds the disease in check and stops its expansion long enough for the tree to compartmentalize it and fight on its own. This kind of treatment will only be effective if the underlying cause, such as a poorly placed

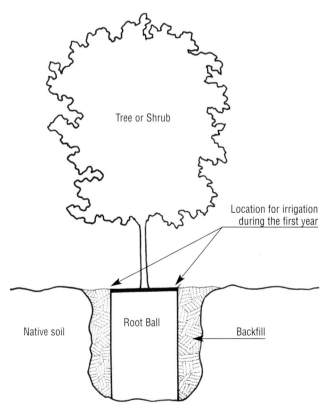

Fig. 2-8: Placing irrigation for first season

sprinkler, is addressed. Sometimes a fungicide treatment cannot save a tree, but it can extend its life significantly enough to make it worth while.

If the root crown rot has exposed an area of inner wood, it is a good idea to paint that exposed area with copper fungicide to reduce the chance of infection by a wood decay fungus.

GIRDLING

What's really going on?

When plants are young, and not properly cared for, they can get girdling roots. This is especially true if, in the nursery, they were left in a container too long or were improperly shifted to a larger container. Girdling roots are roots that rap themselves around the root crown area of the tree.

Fig. 2-9: These roots will eventually cause long-term distress to the tree.

Why it matters:

As these girdling roots grow they put pressure on the trunk. The trunk also puts pressure against the root. Over time the increasing pressure reduces the transport of carbohydrates and photosynthates down to the roots in the inner bark of the tree. This weakens the tree by starving the roots to the extent that the root affects that transport. (Fig. 2-9)

Girdling roots also create a mechanically weak spot in the wood at the location of the girdling. This operates much like a bubble in a piece of glass. It becomes the most likely place for the tree to break if it is put under any stress, say from wind or rain. I have seen otherwise healthy trees break off at the base with just a little bit of wind pressure, due to the damage caused by girdling roots.

What you can do about it:

The most important thing you can do to avoid this problem is to examine trees very closely before purchasing or planting them. Disturb the soil around the root crown and make sure there is no hidden girdling root. If there is a small girdling root or two, ¾ of an inch in diameter, or less, they can be pruned out. Cut them off close to the root crown, and then again outward five or six inches. If there are larger or more numerous girdling roots, choose a different tree. If you have the problem in an existing tree, and the problem is not too advanced, the root can be carefully removed using a chisel. This is best done by a professional arborist. It is probably best not to use an axe in this kind of situation, because it's easy to do additional damage to the root crown of the tree. If the problem is very severe and longstanding, you may want to get a Certified Arborist's opinion. The tree may need to be removed.

age keeps the roots from obtaining the nutrition necessary for their continued growth and sustenance. After a period the visible part of the tree will become weak and discolored. Often, people think this

Fig. 2-10: A moment of carelessness creates a lifelong wound for a tree.

STRING TRIMMERS

What's really going on?

Fig. 2-11: This is a common result of string trimmer damage.

As we discussed earlier in this chapter, the root crown is an important location in the transport of carbohydrates and photosynthates between the root system and the foliage.

Why it matters:

When people use string trimmers to remove grass and weeds from the base of trees, many times they do damage to the outer and inner bark of the tree. Some trees that have thin outer bark and tender inner bark are particularly susceptible to this. Crape Myrtle is a good example. This type of dam-

look is due to a lack of water and nutrients in the soil. It is from a lack of water and nutrients, because the roots have starved and can no longer do their job of transporting water and raw material up to the leaves to make food for the tree. If fifty percent or more of the circumference of the lower trunk is damaged in this way, the tree is doomed. It will die, or at best, never put on additional growth. (Fig. 2-10, 2-11)

This is one of the most serious, yet common tree problems in our urban and suburban landscapes. The sad thing is, it is easily prevented. It is a waste of resources, time and money.

What you can do about it:
The best thing you can do is to keep turf, or other growth, away from the base of your tree. Create a clean area of exposed soil around the base so people won't be tempted

to get close with a string trimmer. (Fig. 2-12) There are protective devices called tree guards, typically made from a plastic tube slit vertically or a roll of plastic, which can be wrapped around the base of the trunk. (Fig. 2-13) This will protect the tree if someone doesn't have the good sense to stay away from it with a string trimmer. The space around the tree can be kept clean by hand weeding, hoeing or spraying with a contact herbicide. If you use a herbicide, make sure not to use it on a tree with green bark. The bark needs to be brown or grey and mature or the herbicide can cause severe damage. If some of the inner wood, the xylem, is exposed by string trimmer damage, you may want to apply a copper fungicide either by painting or spraying. This will inhibit the penetration and establishment of wood-decay fungi.

Fig. 2-12: The simplest way to avoid string trimmer damage. (bare dirt).

Fig. 2-13: Tree guards are inexpensive, simple and fast to apply.

Good timber does not grow with ease; the stronger the wind, the stronger the trees.

— J. Willard Marriott

CHAPTER 3

THE TRUNK
Keeping Straight

The trunk is the connection between the two major systems of a tree. It is the conduit through which flow the raw materials up from the roots and the finished products of photosynthesis down from the canopy. Anything damaging that happens to this area of the tree affects the entire tree. The trunk of a tree is synonymous with strength and endurance. It is in many ways the least active, yet most crucial area of the tree. Without its stout work, a tree would be a mere ground cover or shrub. The bark of many trees has a mixture of colors and textures that creates a subtle beauty unlike that in the rest of the tree. (Fig. 3-1A, B)

Fig. 3-1A: This Strawberry tree bark has a cinnamon color and softly shaggy appearance.

Fig. 3-1B: Cork Oak bark is fascinating to see and touch.

WOOD DECAY

What's really going on?

Wood decay will be a part of the discussion in several places in this book, so it seems wise to discuss it in depth here so later references will make more sense. Anytime inactive wood is exposed to the air or soil there is a good chance it will be infected by a wood decay fungus. You are probably familiar with some of these fungi because of the interesting, and sometimes beautiful, fruiting bodies they cre-

Fig. 3-2: There are many interesting kinds of wood decay conks.

Fig. 3-3: Different types of wood decay prefer different types of wood.

ate. (Fig. 3-2, 3-3) The spores produced by these fungal fruit are like the finest of powders and are carried for miles by the wind. They are ubiquitous, and we are frequently breathing them.

Why it matters:

While we may admire the oddly attractive conks (fruiting bodies), they are busy slowly destroying the structure of the tree. Once a spore attaches itself to an area of exposed wood, it imbeds a very fine root-like structure into the wood. It then continues its invasion of the wood by breaking down the lignin and/or cellulose that gives wood both its strength and flexibility. (Fig. 3-4) These fungi typically do not damage active tissue like the inner phloem, cambium or outer xylem. If there is enough of the healthy, active tissue of a tree surrounding the rotten, inactive tissue, there is no immediate health concern for the

Fig. 3-4: You can see the beginning of decay and weakness in the heartwood of this tree.

tree. Once a tree's structural integrity has been compromised by this turning of wood to mush, a branch or the whole tree can break and cause great damage to itself or anything beneath it. (Fig. 3-5)

What you can do about it:
Avoid making large cuts. Avoid wounding a tree in any way. Avoid exposing any inner wood of the tree. If you must expose wood or have wood exposed by disease, sunscald or other damage, I recommend you treat the exposed area with a copper fungicide. Many copper fungicides are labeled for spraying trees. If the exposed wood is from a new cut, you should wait a few days to a few weeks to let those tissues dry out before applying the copper, because you really do not want the tree to absorb too much copper into its active tissues. A small amount of copper is necessary to plant life, but too much can be poisonous. Absorbing too much copper into the vascular system of a tree could damage it.

SUNSCALDING
What's really going on?
The way that we usually grow trees in urban/suburban areas is to trim them in such a manner that six to ten feet of trunk is exposed.

After trimming there are few, if any, branches growing from the ground up to the base of the canopy. (Fig. 3-6) That is the general vision of what a "proper" tree

Fig. 3-5: Ultimately the strong wood surrounding the decay can no longer hold the weight of the branch.

Fig. 3-6: A tree forced to live within an imaginary vision of what a tree should look like.

looks like. This trimming is an attempt to grow a tree in a way that would rarely take place in nature. In nature, trees will typically grow with their foliage hanging almost all the way to the ground. (Fig. 3-7)

Another problem frequently seen in the Central Valley is the use of trees that are not truly adaptable to our area. We use these trees because of their wonderful attributes but often we find they are not the wisest choice. The Central Valley is hot and dry and species used to that type of environment are the preferred choice.

Why it matters:
The improper trimming of trees often results in scalding of the bark. (Fig. 3-8) It is very like you

or I getting sunburn. Most people keep a good portion of their skin covered for much of the year. If we suddenly expose our skin to prolonged sun, even fifteen to twenty minutes, we can have very damaged skin. Trees, although damaged by sun more slowly, are still damaged. They heal much more slowly. They have the disadvantage of not being able to cover themselves or get out of the sun. Often we use trees that are not appropriate for our environment. These trees may have more tender bark than trees that are native to hot, dry environments like ours. Trees with green bark are usually of this ilk. The scalding usually takes place on the south and west sides of the tree. The scalded bark can no longer function correctly

Fig. 3-7: How a tree protects its trunk and roots from Central Valley sunshine.

Susan Neri

to deliver the goods as we've discussed previously. Scalding wounds almost never heal because the cause is never addressed. These wounds open the tree to insects, disease and wood-decay fungi.

What you can do about it:

The first and best thing to do is to be careful in your choice of tree. Always make sure you know where a species originated and what kind of conditions it is designed to handle. You should be able to discern whether it will be susceptible to sunscald. Another step to avoid sunscald is to not prune the lower branches of a tree too early in the life of the tree. When we examine trees in nature they nearly always have branches hanging near or all the way to the ground. Over a great amount of time, because those lower branches are shaded by branches that grow above them, the tree may choose to jettison the lower branches and let them die off. There is a great amount of variability among species in this facet of growth. This happens because they are less efficient at photosynthesizing due to the decreased light that they receive. Due to this process, many trees in maturity may look somewhat like our idea of an umbrella shaped tree. This

takes a long time and during this time the trunk is only slowly exposed to the sun and becomes rougher and tougher in preparation for that intensified exposure.

When you keep lower branches on a tree, you can cut them short; say four to ten inches from the trunk, with leaves remaining on them. This will protect and thicken the trunk while not allowing those branches to become too large. When we remove a tree's natural shade from its trunk we are doing a disservice to our investment. A tree can be shaded by installing two stakes, a foot or so apart, east and west of each other, on the south side of the tree and stapling some burlap

Fig. 3-8: This is a serious problem that can only be partially remedied, but easily prevented.

or shade cloth between them. Painting the trunk with white paint will reflect some of the damaging light and heat. You should use exterior grade, water-based, latex paint. Exterior grade will last longer. Latex is flexible and water-based paints won't poison a tree like oil-based paints can. If you have sunscald damage you may want to apply copper fungicide to exposed wood. If you are going to paint the trunk white, apply the fungicide before the paint.

MECHANICAL WOUNDING

What's really going on?

Many things wound trees. People carve romantic graffiti on trunks. People hit them with gardening equipment like mowers and string trimmers. (Fig. 3-9) People nail things to them, wrap wire around them, leave stakes and ties on too

> *A tree never hits an automobile except in self-defense.*
> — Author Unknown

long. (Fig. 3-10) All these things wound trunks to a varying degree. Some species can tolerate a fair amount of wounding, but it's never good for a tree. Tree trimmers, who should know better, are another frequent reason for tree injury. Some use spikes or gaffs to climb trees they are supposed to be helping. These spikes are attached to their boots and are jammed into the trunk of the tree to help the climber get around in the tree. The truth is, "real" climbers rarely need spikes. Ladders and ropes are usually sufficient for a tree expert to do the job. Why would someone whose

Fig. 3-9: New damage and scars from old wounds

Fig. 3-10: Trees can grow around foreign objects, but it creates a weak spot in the tree.

Susan Neri

job it is to take care of your trees repeatedly jab the trunk full of spike holes? In unusually dangerous or difficult climbs or when a tree is going to be removed anyway, spikes are useful. Unfortunately, I have seen many cases where a tree trimmer (I use the term loosely) climbed trees of only twenty to thirty feet in height and eight to fourteen inches in trunk diameter using spikes.

Why it matters:

Any wound opens a pathway through which insects and disease may enter. The parts of the bark and wood that are damaged can no longer do their job of transporting water and raw materials upward or photosynthates downward. In the case of trimmers climbing trees with spikes, if the spikes are not sterilized between trees, those spikes can carry disease and inject it right into the tree. This is similar to when people use non-sterile hypodermic needles, passing disease to one another. I have seen trees infected with disease in this way. I've also seen trees where a carpenter worm adult female moth laid her eggs in such a wound and a larva had successfully begun eating a large tunnel in a willow tree. Some insects,

especially carpenter worms, look for wounds made by tree spikes and use these wounds as a receptacle for their eggs. (Fig. 3-11)

What you can do about it:

Always check your tree ties, cables and stakes every six months. Don't nail things to your trees. Make sure you demand that your tree climbers don't use spikes unless absolutely necessary. If they need to, the spikes should be sterilized.

If you have wounding, remove nails and wires when possible. If it is not possible to remove items from a tree without creating much more wounding, remove what part is possible to cut out. The tree will grow around the rest and compartmentalize it. If the wounding has created exposed wood, treat these areas with copper fungicide.

Fig. 3-11: The sawdust-like material you see emerging from the spike hole is frass (waste) from the carpenter worm larvae.

STAKING

What's really going on?

Why do the trees that come from nurseries need to be staked? Why have you never seen a stake on a tree growing in the middle of a forest? The main reason for staking trees is an economic one. In the west we grow most trees in containers. This is for ease of handling and because they are readily available for sale in any season. Even trees grown in containers can grow without stakes, but people like their trees to grow straight. If it's not straight, it won't be sold. Because of this, trees are staked and strapped when grown in containers. (Fig. 3-12) Then, once planted, they must remain staked for some time until they can be weaned off the support.

Why it matters:

This constant relying on the stake by the tree weakens the tree. It is literally a crutch. If the tree is never taught to stand on its own, then when the stake is removed it is wobbly and may fall over immediately or in a high wind. Just like people, unless we are allowed to deal with a certain amount of adversity when young, we will not develop the strength to make it under the future stress of adulthood.

Fig. 3-12: Trees are tightly strapped to the stake, not allowing them the ability to flex.

Fig. 3-13: Note that the tree is held at two points, yet it can still move.

What you can do about it:

If you are planting an already-staked tree in your landscape, you should treat it like a teenager. You need to give it enough wiggle room to gain strength without removing so much support that it breaks in the first tough storm. Practically speaking you should immediately remove the nursery stake. You should always put the side of the tree that was against the stake toward the north. This is because the tissue under the stake has been constantly shaded and is much more susceptible to sunscald as discussed earlier. After removing the nursery stake, install two stout stakes approximately six to ten inches away from the trunk of the tree so that if you drew a line between them it would be perpendicular to the prevailing wind where you live. Then tie the tree to the stakes by using a figure eight loop with one end of the tie around the tree and the other around the stake. Typically, the tie is then nailed to the stake so it will not slide down. It usually takes at least two ties and may take three or four to secure your tree in a straight position between the stakes. This configuration allows your tree to move around in the weather without being bent completely over. (Fig. 3-13. 3-14)

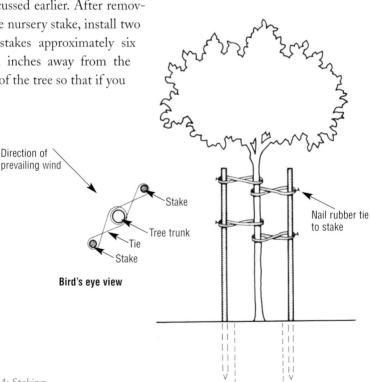

Direction of prevailing wind

Stake

Tree trunk

Tie

Stake

Bird's eye view

Nail rubber tie to stake

Fig. 3-14: Staking

CHAPTER 4

THE BRANCHES
Working Undercover

This, in my opinion is where the true beauty of a tree lies. The branching structure of a healthy, well-pruned tree has an intricate, exquisitely proportional grace of its own. There is nothing more striking than the silhouette of a lacy tree structure against the blue or moonlit sky. (Fig. 4-1)

Fig. 4-1: The history of a tree's life-long dance with the earth and sky sculpted in wood.

CO-DOMINANCE
What's really going on?

In most trees there is a main, upward, branch. It is the dominant branch or leader. Some trees have a more dominant leader and grow in a conical shape, like the classic Christmas tree. Their form is classified as excurrent. Other trees, with a less dominant leader, have a more rounded top, or umbrella-like shape and are classified as decurrent. (Fig. 4-2) The leader stays the leader by somewhat inhibiting the growth of other branches. Imagine a dictator staying in power by inhibiting the ambitions of others. While not appropriate in political affairs, it is appropriate for a tree. The leader inhibits the other limbs by producing a hormone called auxin, which goes throughout the system of the tree. If the top of the leader is cut off, that auxin temporarily stops being produced and the other branches, freed from their imposed inhibition, start growing faster and more upright, vying for dominance. When one finally makes it, the auxin is again produced and the tree settles into its normal habit of growth.

Why it matters:

During the times that branches struggle to replace the leader some of them grow to nearly the same size and height and in the same general direction. (Fig. 4-3, 4-4)

This is called co-dominance. Co-dominance leads to acutely angled crotches where these now important branches attach. Many times bark will be squeezed between these branches in the crotches and tight forks as the branches grow in girth. This creates a weak place, an anomaly, in the structure of the tree, much like a bubble in a piece of glass. It is a likely place for the tree to break if it is put under any stress.

What you can do about it:

The most important thing to do is choose a tree that does not have this tendency and to never top

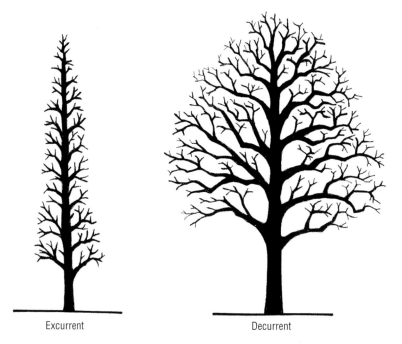

| Excurrent | Decurrent |

Fig. 4-2: Excurrent and decurrent tree shapes

Fig. 4-3: The beginning of trouble. At this point, or before, is when one branch should be pruned.

Fig. 4-4: There is no strength where these two trunks meet.

Fig. 4-5: This branch has an extremely obvious branch collar. Collars on most trees are somewhat less apparent.

your trees. Topping frequently leads to co-dominance and poorly attached branches. If you do experience this situation, one of the co-dominant leaders should be pruned out or cut back substantially, so that the remaining branch can grow more vigorously.

COLLARS AND COMPARTMENTALIZATION
What's really going on?

Where a branch meets another branch, or the trunk, a collar is formed. The collar is the widened area where the attachment occurs. It can be obvious on some species and nearly nonexistent on others. (Fig. 4-5)

Trees have a unique way of defending themselves from disease and insects. It is called compartmentalization. When a branch is cut off, starting at that point, an internal inverted cone of tissue becomes hardened within the tree. This hardening is the result of the tree filling minute spaces with resins and other compounds. This cone shape starts its wide area at the edge of the cut or broken branch. This wide part of the inverted cone is made smaller if the cut is properly made at the outer end of the collar, thus reducing the entire area of compartmentalization or possible decay. The cone then flows in and down through the collar and into the trunk, or larger branch, to its point. (Fig. 4-6)

Why it matters:

This unique area of hardened wood, like an internal scab, makes it harder for insects and disease to penetrate through a broken or cut branch. This is especially important in slowing invasion by wood-decay fungi. The spores of such fungi, which are ubiquitous in the air for much of the year, land on cuts and wounds and eat their way into the heart of a tree. They destroy cellulose and lignin as they go, turning the once hard wood to mushy pulp.

What you can do about it:

When pruning, try to always make your cuts on the branch outside the collar. If you cut into the collar, you create a larger wound. The closer you cut through the collar to the trunk or larger branch, the greater the base of the inverted cone will be. This, in turn, creates a wider, deeper area outside of the compartmentalization, exposing more of the tree to

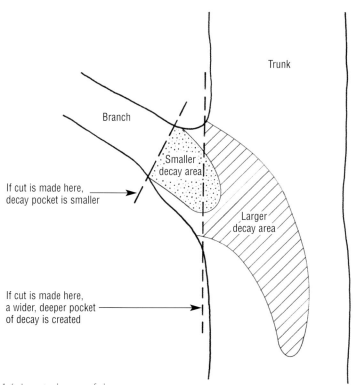

Fig. 4-6: Inverted cone of decay

decay and the probability of disease and insect invasion. (Fig. 4-7) If the tree cannot respond quickly enough with sufficient quantities of resin, the internal protection of compartmentalization will not stop opportunistic, tree destroying, organisms. If you make any cuts two inches or larger in diameter, it is probably wise to treat those cuts either by spraying or painting them with copper fungicide. It is best to let the exposed tissues of the cut dry for a few days to a few weeks before applying the copper. The wait is to avoid having your tree absorb the copper into its system. It will still control any fungus that has been on the surface for that short time.

BRANCH DIEBACK
What's really going on?

What's going on is just what it sounds like. Not all branches dying back on a tree are the result of a problem. There are two types of dieback. One type is when the branches die on the inside of the tree's canopy. The other is when they die on the outside of the canopy.

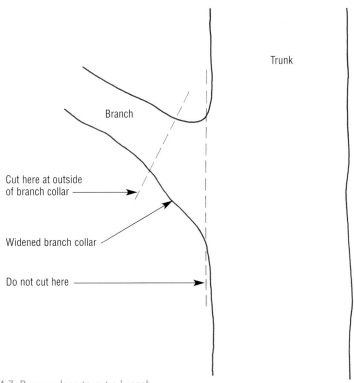

Fig. 4-7: Proper place to cut a branch

Why it matters:

Inside dieback is typically due to a redistribution of the tree's resources to more efficient outer foliage. The branches on the inside of the tree are shaded by outer branches and do not photosynthesize very well. This is a natural, normal occurrence. (Fig. 4-8)

Dieback on the outer canopy of a tree is usually a sign of disease, insect infestation, or environmental stress. (Fig. 4-9, 4-10) If a tree loses more water through its leaves than it can gather through its roots, the tissues will collapse and burn. Trees transpire through small pores in their leaves called stoma. This process is similar to perspiration in humans, but with different mechanisms and functions.

What to do about it:

If the dieback is of the natural, appropriate kind, trimming out the dead wood may be desirable, but is not necessary. If insects or disease causes the problem, a diagnosis needs to be made and the appropriate treatment prescribed. Most insects and some diseases can be treated by injecting the tree, or in some cases the soil.

Fig. 4-8: These dead branches are being jettisoned by the tree.

Fig. 4-9: This dieback on a Raywood Ash tree is caused by a fungus disease.

Fig. 4-10: This dieback on a Chinese Pistache tree is caused by root damage due to excessive moisture in the soil.

Fig. 4-11: Specialized equipment and training is required for this type of injection. The needle on this device goes through the outer bark to the area between the phloem and xylem.

Fig. 4-12: These beetle larvae are called flathead borers. Note the amount of destroyed inner bark carved away by their appetite and the sawdust-like waste, or frass, left behind.

Fig. 4-13: This Maple suffered severe damage from carpenter worms.

(Fig. 4-11) This is a more efficient, effective and less dangerous method than spraying. It is probably best to hire a tree doctor, who is usually a Certified Arborist, with training in tree pests, to diagnose and treat the problem.

If the problem is environmental stress, the first question that should be asked is, "Is this an appropriate tree for this location?" (See Chapter 6 — "Coastal Redwoods in an Inland Environment") If environmental stress is the problem, you may have to increase water, aeration, create shade, treat the soil or spray the tree with anti-transpirant to get it back on the right track.

WOOD BORING INSECTS

What's really going on?

Wood boring insects are the most destructive insects to trees. Many other kinds of insects attack and infest trees, but wood boring insects can literally attack at the heart of a tree. Most boring insects are the larvae of beetles but some are the larvae, or adults, of other types of insects. (Fig. 4-12, 4-13)

Typically, the female of the tree boring species lays her eggs in a crevice on the bark of the target tree. The eggs hatch and the larvae eat their way into the tree. Some species eat their way around just under the outer bark and some go deep into the wood, and still others will eat through both bark and wood. The larvae become pupae, often in the tree, and after a time emerge as adults to mate, lay eggs, and start the cycle all over again. Some wood boring insects repeat this cycle only once a year, others repeat it as many times as they can during appropriate weather.

Termites usually only attack trees in the dry, inactive wood. (Fig. 4-14) Their favorite entry points are where large cuts have been made or in broken branches and other wounds.

Why it matters:

When wood boring insects eat the phloem or inner bark tissue, it stops the flow of carbohydrates to the roots. When they destroy xylem, or wood tissue, it stops the flow of water and raw materials to the canopy. Of course, when they eat both types of tissue it is doubly destructive. Wood boring insects can also introduce disease directly into the system of a tree, and the holes they make are open to infection by air-borne disease. Many trees die each year due to the damage of wood boring insects.

Dry wood termites don't disrupt the flow of water and raw materials because they live in the inner inactive wood, but they weaken the structural integrity of the tree, and can contribute to it becoming a hazard.

If you are finding holes in the bark of your tree that are in a nearly straight line circling the branch or trunk, the culprit is a sapsucking woodpecker. Although they can cause damage to a tree, it is seldom as damaging as wood boring insects. (Fig. 4-15)

Fig. 4-14: Although there is some borer damage in the outer wood of this tree, the multiple small caverns of destruction in the inner wood are due to dry wood termites.

Fig. 4-15: No boring insects are capable of planning to exit the tree in a nearly straight line, so this kind of damage is due to sapsuckers.

What you can do about it:
The best defense against boring insects is to keep your tree well watered and healthy. Boring insects look for, and can more easily attack, weakened or stressed trees. My wife says the best defense is to teach them to have a sense of humor.

With these types of insects, timing of any spray is critical because once they are inside the tree, a spray will not reach them. You have to try to treat them when the adult females will be landing on the trees to lay eggs. It is imperative to understand the life cycle of the specific pest you have a problem with. This is such a difficult challenge that I usually don't recommend trying it. It can be a misuse of pesticides.

Annual soil or intracambial injections of a systemic insecticide, that is labeled for that particular kind of application, can be the best way to prophylactically treat the tree to avoid most borers. Once the tree is systemically treated, when the larvae start to eat their way into the tree, the insecticide present in the tree's system kills them before they can do significant damage. Different insecticides kill different families of insects, so you must know which critter you are trying to exterminate. For instance, carpenter worm, a common pest of willow trees in hot dry climates, will not be killed by an injection of imidacloprid, which works well on most other boring insects, especially beetles.

Termites can be avoided by an annual painting of large open wounds with a copper fungicide/insecticide mix. The copper is to slow decay of the wood and the insecticide is to kill the termites. They can be treated after they inhabit the tree, but only as deeply into the wood as the pesticide will reach.

OVER-PRUNING AND TOPPING

What's really going on?
You've seen it — a tree that looks like a hat rack, a porcupine, a club, a stump. (Fig. 4-16, 4-17, 4-18) Some people consider this tree trimming. It's really tree abuse. Trees often can benefit from pruning. In an urban/suburban environment where we cram them into yards and commercial locations, trimming may become a necessity. Tree trimming can also be used to make a tree healthier, and ornamentally or aesthetically more pleasing to its owner. Even so, topping and over-pruning are not only damaging to trees, but

also ill advised for tree owners, more costly, and just plain ugly.

Why it matters:

A tree's canopy is designed to create a specific amount of carbohydrates and other photosynthates for use by the rest of the tree, particularly the roots. When more than twenty percent of the green canopy of a tree is removed, it starts to have negative effects on various parts of the tree. If most of the canopy is removed those effects are amplified and more problems are created.

When too much canopy is removed, the roots begin to be starved for carbohydrates. This means they are working less effectively and the canopy is less likely to receive its appropriate amount of raw materials and water. This can shock a tree and start a dangerous downward spiral of reactions. One reaction is for the tree to call up some of its stored carbohydrates and turn them into new canopy as quickly as possible. This results in buds that ordinarily would have remained dormant, creating shoots in places that branches would not ordinarily grow. The resulting branches are an ugly mass of multi-directional shoots that are poorly attached to the branch they sprouted from.

Fig. 4-16: This pruning was so business signs behind the trees could be more easily seen. I would think twice about doing business with someone who would do this to a tree, instead of letting the canopy grow above line of sight to the signs.

Fig. 4-17: Unfortunately, this is what passes for tree trimming too much of the time.

Fig. 4-18: Note the multiple leader response the two trees on the left had from previous topping. The person who trimmed these trees is clueless. Why not get it over with and just remove them?

Fig. 4-19: This is an example of why it is not only bad for the tree, but a waste of time and money to top or over-prune your trees.

I've heard it said that people prune trees back to the nubs so they won't have to rake the leaves during the fall. This is insane. It takes a huge amount of labor, money, and trips to, and fees at, the dump to prune a tree like this in a regular fashion. It is economically impractical. And, I'll say it one more time...it's ugly!

What you can do about it:
Obviously, do not over-prune your trees. If you intend to prune the tree yourself, obtain information on pruning correctly. Take a class or go on the web and examine information at a site such as the one belonging to the International Society of Arboriculture to learn the correct methods of pruning. (Fig. 4-20, 4-21)

(Fig. 4-19) In the future they will be a tangled mess and are much more likely to break off, possibly causing harm and owner liability. The roots, being stressed by this temporary starvation, are more susceptible to attack by disease.

The larger and more numerous cuts caused by this type of pruning result in a much greater chance of infection by wood decay fungi and dry wood termites. When a tree's canopy is removed, it's as if you or I took off our shirt and stood in the sun for day after day, exposing our, until-recently-shaded skin, to harsh UV radiation. We would fry. So does a tree. Its skin, the bark, is burned creating sunscalded areas where disease and insects can more readily prey on the tree. (See Chapter 3 — "Sunscalding")

If you are going to hire someone to prune your tree, make sure to hire a true professional. It will be more expensive than some fellow driving around your neighborhood with a pick-up and a chainsaw, but you wouldn't take your sick child to the butcher for an operation, just because it cost less in the short run. If you can, hire a company with a Certified Arborist or Certified Tree Worker on staff. No matter who you hire, ask for references. Call them and visit past pruning sites to look at the type of trimming the company does. Remember that your trees are a huge, long-term investment. Many people don't realize that a well-pruned tree should look natural. It's like a good hair cut; only the owner and the tree trimmer should know for sure that it was trimmed. If a tree is correctly pruned, over time it will actually require less, not more, pruning. More beauty, less work, less money…it makes sense!

Fig. 4-20: Notice that the canopy and even some interior branches remain. The look stays natural.

Fig. 4-21: It's hard to tell anything has been done to this tree. That's the idea.

MISTLETOE

What's really going on?

Mistletoe is a plant, plant parasite, meaning, it is a plant that is a parasite on other plants, usually trees. The kind of mistletoe discussed in this section is the common broad leaf mistletoe. It is found in many species of trees. It roots into the trees' branches and sucks up water and raw materials from the tree. It is as if the host tree were its soil. Mistletoe is green and photosynthesizes much like the trees it inhabits. Once the ball of mistletoe reaches about eighteen inches in diameter, it will start flowering and producing seed. The seeds are spread by falling from the cluster and by birds. (Fig. 4-22)

Fig. 4-22: It may mean a kiss at Christmas for you, but it may mean the kiss of death for your tree.

Why it matters:

When mistletoe is attached to a branch, it reduces the amount of water and raw materials that will flow past it to the leaves of that branch. This reduces the ability of that branch to create food for itself and the rest of the tree. Mistletoe also makes it much more difficult for a tree to get water to its leaves when under drought stress. If there is a limited supply of water and the mistletoe is getting a portion of it, there is that much less remaining for the tree. If there is enough mistletoe in a tree, the tree can be sucked dry and die, which in turn kills the mistletoe too. That's what happens to greedy parasites. Does that make you think of anyone you know? Oops, back to mistletoe. In my experience, trees with mistletoe frequently have other problems, like wood boring insects or scale. It seems a weak tree is more susceptible to mistletoe, and a mistletoe infested tree is more susceptible to other pests.

What you can do about it:

There are three methods of attacking a mistletoe problem, and they can be used in conjunction. First, the most effective way to remove mistletoe is just that, remove it. Cut the entire section of branch that the mistletoe is attached to, cutting at least a foot or so behind where the parasite is attached. If the mistletoe is attached to a major scaffold branch, the main trunk, or another important branch you must keep to maintain the integrity of the tree, you can block light from getting to it. The best way to do this is to cut the mistletoe out of the tree, back to where it is attached. Then wrap the area, a foot above, and a foot below the attachment point with black plastic, thick enough to keep light from hitting the area. A large black trash bag is appropriate for the job. In the case of mistletoe attached to an important branch, or if it is too high to reach for pruning, spraying it may be a useful alternative. There is a product called Florel that is labeled to treat mistletoe. It is created from a concentrated form of a naturally occurring plant hormone. When this hormone is sprayed on the mistletoe, as directed on the product label, it can burn the mistletoe out of the tree without harming the tree. This type of application should be done on deciduous trees during their leafless season.

> *And on the banks, on both sides of the river, there will grow all kinds of trees for food. Their leaves will not wither nor their fruit fail, but they will bear fresh fruit every month, because the water for them flows from the sanctuary. Their fruit will be for food, and their leaves for healing.*
>
> — Ezekiel 47:12

CHAPTER 5

THE CANOPY
Show Me the Green

This is where one of the most amazing and possibly one of the most important events on earth takes place, photosynthesis. It is the turning of warm sunlight into life-giving sugar, wood and medicine. It is the way we harvest the energy of the sun. Nearly all life on Earth owes its existence to this miracle that takes place in the leaves of plants. The vast forests that have existed on this planet for ages make it possible for us to have the opportunity to care for them and us. There is a truly deep and critical connection between them and us. Without trees, we would have a meager existence at best, if at all.

A tree is designed to receive the maximum amount of sunlight on its leaves' surfaces. Trees are extremely phototropic, meaning they are strongly driven to seek out and adjust themselves to the available light. A tree actually moves itself and its leaves throughout a day and throughout its life to catch the maximum amount of sunlight. The amazing process of photosynthesis takes carbon out of the air, and with the energy of the sun, combines it with oxygen and hydrogen to create glucose. Glucose is a sugar, a form of carbohydrate that can then be broken down to release energy or utilized to create more tree parts. It can be combined in the tree with other elements to create useful phytochemicals. This process, called photosynthesis, produces the sugars that are necessary for the survival of all of the animals on the planet.

The canopy of a tree is a continuous and complex miracle that takes place silently and relentlessly around us every day. We need to do what we can to safeguard that process and that is what this chapter is about. Besides, don't you want the shade?

SUCKING INSECTS
What's really going on?

For trees, sucking insects are the most common and most tedious insect problem. Examples of sucking insects are such things as aphids, scale, mealy bugs, thrips, white fly, leafhoppers, sharpshooters, lace bugs, and psyllid. Some of these insects are mobile and some are usually stationary. They pierce the tissue of plants with their mouthparts and suck juices out of the plant. Some suck juices out of leaf tissue, some out of smaller stems and some pierce far enough to suck juices out of the wood. (Fig. 5-1, 5-2, 5-3, 5-4)

Fig. 5-1: Aphids on the back of Maple leaves.

Fig. 5-2: The small tan and grey circular spots on this Alder tree's bark are Walnut scale. Very insidious because they are hard to detect.

Fig. 5-3: The freckle-like spots on Sycamore leaves are a tip-off that the tree has Sycamore scale. The fuzzy white spots are also a clear sign.

Fig. 5-4: These white tent-like structures are the home of Red Gum Lerp psyllids. They are made out of crystallized sugar, which is the waste of the insect.

In the basic life cycle of these insects, the female often lays her eggs on the surface of leaves or stems. When the temperature and conditions are right the insects will hatch and go through some larval or nymphal stages, depending on the species of insect. Larvae molt their old skin as they grow, then pupate, and emerge as an adult. This is similar to the process most people are familiar with in butterflies, but the larvae of butterflies are not sucking insects. Nymphs look much like an adult, but without wings. They continue to grow, molting their skin until adulthood. Most of the sucking insects go through this nymphal process. The nymphs are also known as instars.

These sucking insects can do damage in the nymphal stage, the adult stage, or often both. They tap into the tree, often in the leaves, usually in the phloem, and sometimes in the xylem, and then suck sap out of the tree. After the sap has been processed through the insect, it is excreted in what is called honeydew, a euphemism for bug excrement. Actually, it is sweet. Some people in various parts of the world use the crystallized form of this honeydew to sweeten their hot drinks, yum!

Why it matters:
If there are only a few sucking insects on a tree, there is no cause for alarm. However, if there are many it can seriously jeopardize the tree's health. The insects are tapping into the tree's carbohydrates and if enough insects are present, it can greatly stress the tree. In essence, starving and overworking it, keeping the right amount of carbohydrates from reaching the roots. If there are enough xylem-sucking insects, such as sharpshooters, they can wilt a tree.

Another problem caused by these types of insects is the spread of disease. Their mouthparts operate like miniature hypodermic needles. Most of the insects have to discharge saliva into the plant tissue to create a sort of vacuum in their body. This vacuum enables them to suck sap back in. In the process they may have sucked up a disease in a different plant and discharged it into a new host plant.

A black fungus called black sooty mold often grows on the excreted honeydew that builds up on the leaves. This side effect of sucking insects can somewhat inhibit light reception in the leaf, therefore reducing photosynthesis. The physical damage that some insects do to leaves, especially young leaves, can cause them to callus, twist and become deformed. This also reduces the plants ability to photosynthesize.

One of the first signs of a tree with sucking insects is a continuous flow of ants up and down the trunk. These ants are taking advantage of the available "sugar water" and using it as a food source. Many times, they will have discovered a camouflaged colony of sucking insects way up in your tree where you cannot see them. With this food source, the ants can increase the size of their colony, lucky you, and in addition, take an active role in protecting the sucking insects from beneficial insects that would prey on them and help you out.

What you can do about it:

If the problem is small, you may be able to rid yourself of most of the insects with a simple washing of the leaves and small stems, using a high-pressure nozzle on the end of a garden hose. If this doesn't work you may want to try a soap-type insecticide labeled for these insects. Horticultural oils can be effective at controlling sucking insects. There are some

newer insecticides and insect repellents made from the volatile oils of such things as thyme, cedar, cinnamon, and clove. These repellents are usually harmless to humans, but do a good job of either driving away or killing insects.

Another way to decrease the sucking insect population is to purchase and promote beneficial insects. These insects either prey on, or parasitize, the insects that are causing your problem. They can be purchased from some nurseries or beneficial insectaries. A good way to find an insectary is to go online.

If the problem is larger and the trees are becoming truly debilitated, it is best to apply a systemic insecticide labeled for such use. (Fig. 5-5) It will travel throughout the vascular system of the tree,

Fig. 5-5: Appropriately used, a soil injection has less chance of non-target contamination. Special equipment is necessary.

usually killing all of the insects. Start with a systemic insecticide that is the least toxic to humans and pets. Systemic insecticides are best applied by a trunk or soil injection. Soil injections are the best because they don't require holes to be drilled in the tree. The trunk injection is the most direct method of applying an insecticide to only the "patient" being treated. Often a systemic treatment, done correctly, will give yearlong protection. Injections avoid the problem of dangerous spray drift landing in undesirable places, and the need for frequent reapplications. Injections are also much less damaging to any beneficial insects. Spraying for insects has become almost obsolete in recent years, and is used only in limited situations. If you need to have a tree injected or sprayed, it is best to hire a pest control person trained in tree problems or an arborist trained in pest control.

Fig. 5-6: These caterpillars create a massive amount of soft, silky webbing.

Susan Neri

CHEWING INSECTS
What's really going on?

Examples of chewing insects are caterpillars, grasshoppers, and the larvae and adults of some beetles and other classes of insects. The damage they do is easy to understand. They chew off and eat parts of a tree's leaves. This damage deforms the leaf making it less able to do its job.

Why it matters:

The number one reason this matters is that there is an immediate reduction in leaf surface available for photosynthesis. Any deformation caused by chewing reduces optimum photosynthesis. The chewed edges of leaves are wounds that are open to infection by air-borne diseases. The insects themselves can carry a disease and infect a tree. A classic example of this is the Dutch elm disease carried by the elm beetle. If the attacking insects are tent creating caterpillars, the tent webbing they create can obscure light from the leaves.(Fig. 5-6) In addition to all of these serious problems, chewing insects can reduce the aesthetic value of a tree.

What you can do about it:

There are a variety of techniques to destroy or control these insects.

High pressure water, soap type insecticides, beneficial predatory and parasitic insects, horticultural or volatile oil sprays, and systemics can all be used to great effect. If you try the high-pressure water method, you must be disciplined in the regularity with which you spray off the trees or it won't be effective. Just as with sucking insects, you will want to spray the pests off of the tree when you notice them starting to build up in number, but before they can do too much damage.

For certain chewing insects such as caterpillars and grasshoppers, there is a class of insecticide called a B.t. B.t. is the result of modified bacteria, which creates a toxin that only kills specific classes of insects and is completely harmless to plants, other classes of insects or humans and pets.

FUNGAL LEAF DISEASES
What's really going on?

Many fungi attack leaves. Sometimes they gang together and attack leaves in teams. Sometimes they cause small discolored spots on leaves, and at other times they completely destroy the leaves and kill small stems and branches. Examples of common leaf attacking fungi are anthracnose, powdery mildew, and downy mildew. (Fig. 5-7, 5-8) Leaf fungi typically start from a hard to destroy spore. Often this spore is blown by the wind and lands on the tree. It can be there because the disease is already present on another part of the tree, a neighbor's tree, or a tree miles away. Sometimes birds, insects and even man can move fungus problems from one tree to another. When weather conditions are appropriate, the spore that has quietly been

Fig. 5-7: Anthracnose on a Modesto Ash causes damaged tissue, deformation and leaf drop.

Fig. 5-8: Sycamores in California are regularly plagued with anthracnose.

waiting on the surface of the leaf will peg down into the leaf. It then begins to grow what is called hyphae or mycelium. Hyphae are super fine hair-like structures. Many times these fungal filaments will form mats that are visible to the unaided eye. That is the mycelium. During the process the fungus extracts the nutrients it requires from the leaf, destroying tissue as it does. When the fungus reaches a certain stage of maturity, it creates more spores that are spread around the environment near and far to continue its process of destruction.

Why it matters:

Leaf fungi, while destroying the leaf tissue, reduces the tree's ability to photosynthesize. They also rob the leaves directly of their nutrients. Many trees with leaves damaged by leaf attacking fungi will jettison those leaves, creating a mess in your yard and a crisis for the tree. The tree has to use a great deal of stored carbohydrates from the wood and roots to refoliate. This refoliation temporarily can starve other systems in the plant, such as the roots. The process is very taxing on the tree. If the disease is not controlled and this process takes place several times, it can actually kill the tree, or at least weaken it enough to allow some other more deadly foe, or a combination of attackers, to kill the tree.

What you can do about it:

The best method to avoid a leaf fungus problem is to choose a tree that is not prone to such diseases. If you don't have that luxury, or you desire that kind of a tree anyway, there are some treatments. If the weather is dry enough where you live and your tree is otherwise healthy it may be best just to suffer through a small amount of leaf drop and disease on your tree. Often, trees with such diseases can tolerate a moderate amount of the problem. If the disease becomes an issue the tree can either be sprayed or injected. The spray should be a fungicide specifically labeled for the tree and disease you have. It should also cover as much leaf surface as possible. Some diseases, like anthracnose in a sycamore tree can be treated systemically with a trunk injection. This takes specialized equipment and expertise and would require a licensed applicator. Typically, any fungicidal application will not eradicate the disease, but only control it, giving your tree a break so it can recover from the stress.

BACTERIAL LEAF DISEASES

Bacterial leaf diseases operate like leaf fungal diseases. They get their life and nutrition by robbing from your tree. Probably the best known bacterial disease that affects the leaves of trees is fire blight. (Fig. 5-9)

What's really going on?
Much like a fungus, bacteria can survive during tough times in the form of a hard to kill spore. When conditions are right, this spore starts to grow and divide and insert itself into your tree. There it continues to divide and invade the cells of the tree, devouring the components of the cells and destroying them.

Why it matters:
The result of this invasion is a wholesale destruction of leaves and smaller branches in the canopy. This, of course, reduces photosynthesis. If it goes on long enough and destroys enough tissue, it can actually kill a tree, because the roots will starve to death and be unable to defend themselves from soil borne invaders.

What you can do about it:
In the case of fire blight, it is possible to choose trees that are less

Fig. 5-9: Classic symptoms of fire blight.

susceptible or not susceptible. Flowering Pears, Crabapples, Photinias, and Loquats are very susceptible to fire blight.

Immediately upon the realization that you have such a disease, prune out the affected parts. You must prune well below where you see the disease, making a cut into healthy tissue. After each cut, and before the next, you should sterilize your pruning equipment with a ten percent chlorine bleach solution, or full strength rubbing alcohol.

It may also be advisable to spray your tree with a dormant spray containing a copper fungicide during winter. Some applicators also apply an antibiotic spray at bloom time as a preventative or anytime the tree shows the disease.

CHAPTER 6

OTHER PROBLEMS AND ADDITIONAL INFORMATION

This chapter contains some important, practical information that did not fall neatly into the prior chapters. The following topics are really less about the bad things that can happen to your trees and more about some of the side effects of living with trees and how we manage them and interface with them in concrete ways.

SPONTANEOUS LIMB DROP

What's really going on?

Occasionally, and for no apparent reason, a limb comes crashing down. It has no obvious signs of disease, insect damage, or structural weakness. It just falls. This can be very disconcerting, especially if you or your house or car is

underneath the tree at the time. This problem exists all over the world. There are arborists everywhere looking into it. I have heard several theories for the cause, but none that have been widely accepted as of yet. This event usually takes place toward the end of summer, and usually in the afternoon or evening. There is obviously some change in the relationship between temperature, transpiration, turgidity, weight of the limb, and flexibility of tissue at work here, but exactly what it is remains to be determined. There are certain trees common to our landscapes that seem more susceptible than others are. Some of them are liquidambar, Deodar Cedar, many species of eucalyptus, and some oaks. In other parts of the world, other species also have this problem.

Why it matters:
It matters because, of course, it can cause great damage to home and possessions, not to mention life and limb.

What you can do about it:
The most effective thing you can do is not plant a tree that is known to suffer from this problem. If you still want a tree of a suspect species (some of which are great trees in most other respects), or if you already have one, there are still some things you can do.

Don't have a picnic, or park your car, immediately under the tree, especially in the summer. Make sure your homeowners insurance is current, just in case someone does park themselves or their vehicle under your tree. Hire a competent arborist or tree trimmer to gently thin your tree

I think that I shall never see a billboard lovely as a tree. Perhaps, unless the billboards fall, I'll never see a tree at all.

— Ogden Nash,
Song of the Open Road, 1933

making sure that there is a little less weight on the ends of the major branches. Making appropriate, arboriculturally correct cuts should do this. Make sure your tree is healthy in every other way, with sufficient fertilization and water.

NUISANCE FRUIT CONTROL
What's really going on?
Almost every tree, with the exception of some hybrids, has fruit of one sort or another. Some trees that are planted for their flowers or other beauty, when mature, may have fruit that becomes a problem for the owner and others. Some examples of common trees with this problem are Flowering Pears, Flowering Plums, Flowering Crabapples, liquidambars, mulberries, and olives.

Why it matters:
These trees can create so much fruit that it can make a huge mess on your property or on your neighbor's property. The smashed fruit can often be tracked into a home or building and stain the carpeting. They can stain cars, sidewalks, and buildings. Birds may eat the fruit and deposit the reconstituted, still-stain-creating fruit on various parts of your

buildings and property. The fruit can be slippery, or in the case of liquidambars, kind of like walking on big spiky marbles, both of which can cause you, or a person looking for a good law suit, to fall and injure themselves.

What you can do about it:
The easiest thing to do, of course, is don't plant that species of tree. If you want the tree and the landscape is new or you don't mind changing it, you can plant a thick ground cover under the tree where the fruit can fall and can cause no problem. If you already have one of these trees over a walkway you can spray them to control the fruit. The most common type of spray is a plant hormone. These are naturally occurring in many plants. For the purposes of spraying they are synthetically created in a concentrated form. They are sprayed onto the tree, most often during the peak of the bloom. Once absorbed they induce the creation of another hormone that will abscise the flowers and fruit, leaving you with a nearly fruitless tree come next summer or fall. The other method of control by chemical application is by use of a plant growth regulator. This man-made compound causes the tree to slow its growth to such an extent

that the flowers and/or fruit never grow or become mature. Although the hormone type controls can be purchased retail, I suggest that the most effective result from use of either chemical application would be gained by hiring a licensed applicator with the appropriate equipment, experience and knowledge. Some trees can be kept from fruiting by pruning them severely. I don't suggest this method of nuisance fruit control because it is too damaging to the tree. (See Chapter 4).

OAK GALLS
What's really going on?
Oak galls are a common site on oak trees, especially native oak trees. They occur on other non-indigenous oak trees as well. Most oak galls are usually small deformities that are found on the leaves or stems of the tree, typically on the backs of the leaves and on smaller stems. Galls come in a huge variety. Some take the form of a small turban, some look like small multi-pointed red and white stars; others are small round balls only two millimeters across. There are galls that wiggle like Mexican jumping beans, when they fall to the ground. Other galls resemble a small patch of tan teddy bear fuzz. (Fig. 6-1, 6-2, 6-3, 6-4) Stem

galls are usually a widened-out area of the stem, although some look like green or brown golf balls. Oaks are not the only plants that have galls, but they are amongst the most noticeable. Most oak galls are caused by a particular genus of wasp. These wasps are minute in size. As adults, they are smaller than a gnat. The adult female stings the leaf or stem of the tree and inserts an egg into the tree's tissue. The wasp induces unusual growth in the tissue of the tree and that forms the gall. The wasp's larvae live feed and pupate inside the gall. It eventually hatches out of the gall through a small hole, mates and begins the process over again. Sometimes these wasps alternate the kinds of galls they create with every other generation so the first and third generations create the same kind of gall and the second and fourth generations create an entirely different type of gall.

Why it matters:

It doesn't really matter most of the time. In some instances there may be enough galls on a tree too limit photosynthesis somewhat and possibly use a significant amount of photosynthates that the tree would have otherwise used itself.

Julie McGuinness

Fig. 6-1: Galls come in a wide variety of shapes and sizes.

Julie McGuinness

Fig. 6-2: Galls can be bizarre structures indeed.

Julie McGuinness

Fig. 6-3: Stem galls are frequently less noticed that leaf galls.

Fig. 6-4: This is wooly gall on Southern Live Oak.

What you can do about it:
Most of the time, you shouldn't waste your time doing anything about it. If you believe that the gall wasp infestation is causing your tree any serious problem, hire a professional to examine the situation. If action is warranted, some systemic insecticide injections can impede the infestation. A compound labeled for such a use must be available to make this possible and professional application is probably wise.

COASTAL REDWOODS IN INLAND AREAS
What's really going on?
Coastal Redwood trees, *Sequoia sempervirens*, especially the Aptos Blue and Soquel varieties have become very popular in Califor-

nia, even in the inland valleys, especially the Central Valley. (Fig. 6-5) They are native to the central and north coasts of California. They are useful and beautiful trees with a relatively unique growth habit for trees in urban and suburban settings. There is great risk planting these trees in an inland valley. In most cases on the coast, these trees grow in groups where they can shade each other. In the summer on the coast, there is frequent fog in the morning and the temperatures rarely get much above 90° Fahrenheit because of the influence of the ocean. Even when temperatures are high during the day, it cools off rapidly once the sun sets. There is higher humidity on the coast. The typical soils where these trees are native to are forest soils, with a lower pH, good drainage, and high in organic matter. All these attributes are quite dissimilar to those usually found in inland valleys, with their high summer temperatures lasting late into the night, no summer fog, low humidity, and poorly-drained, slightly alkaline soils, which are low in organic matter. Frequently redwoods are planted in such a way that they do not shade each other and in urban/suburban settings receive much reflected light

Fig. 6-5: A row of healthy Coastal Redwoods.

and heat from asphalt, concrete, and most damaging of all, from swimming pools.

Why it matters:
When redwoods are planted in the Central Valley they find their living conditions very different from those conditions that they were genetically programmed to live in. This environmental stress causes the tissues of the leaves and small branches to burn. The low humidity along with continuous high temperatures are the main causes of this. Sequoias receive the most brutal beating when they are planted on the north and east sides of a swimming pool. The pool acts like a mirror, nearly doubling the sun's energy that reaches the trees. Redwoods are also quite sensitive to chlorine in the air, water or soil, which exacerbates the problems.

What you can do about it:
The best way to avoid these problems is, obviously, not plant Sequoias in an inland area. The best remedy to the issues that arise if you have planted them, is to water your Sequoias substantially in the warm season. Sequoias do not send out as many large searching roots as other kinds of trees. Their roots are smaller and more

numerous in a smaller area. As the trees grow larger, the surface area of leaves exposed to the dry air is increased exponentially. You must increase the water you apply to the same basic area each year as the tree grows larger. Many people apply the same amount of water year after year, thinking that the redwoods mine water farther and farther from the tree, which they do, but slowly. They typically add more roots in the same basic area. This leads to the trees growing well the first five to ten years and then tissue collapses and burns during a hot summer or two.

If you are increasing the water every year and you have a heavy soil typical to inland valleys, you may end up with a soil without enough aeration. Applying products such as John & Bob's Soil Optimizer or Gypsum and installing aeration devices can counteract this problem (See Chapter 1).

TRANSPORTING TREES
What's really going on?
I can't tell you how many times I've been on a highway and seen someone blasting down the road with trees and plants hanging out of the back of a truck, or worse, standing up in the back of a truck. I just think "What a waste of an investment." It is asking for trou-

ble, especially in our hot, dry, climate to transport trees in this manner.

Why it matters:

As the airflow created by the movement of the vehicle goes by the leaves of the tree, it pulls out water from the leaf tissues. It pulls out the moisture faster than the tree can replace it. The cells and vascular tissues dry out and collapse. The leaves turn brown or black and fall off. The plant may or may not recover from such a situation, depending on how much damage has been done. If it does recover, it will still be somewhat set back. The newer and more tender the foliage, the faster you drive, and the hotter and dryer it is, the more severe the damage will be.

What you can do about it:

If you must drive with an exposed tree, and you're not going too far, go thirty-five miles per hour or less. With a very tender tree on a hot day, twenty-five miles per hour can be too fast. The best policy is to place the trees in an enclosed truck or trailer. Also, tarping the foliage of the tree will do the job. Shade cloth is a great material for this kind of job. It doesn't catch the air like a solid tarp, yet diverts so much of the airflow that it protects the plant. If you have small enough shrubs or trees, placing them forward in the bed toward the cab is better than having them ride in back by the tailgate.

USING MEDITERRANEAN CLIMATE TREES

What's really going on?

There are five parts of the world that have what is known as a Mediterranean climate. They include a section of Chile, part of Australia, part of South Africa, and of course, the Mediterranean. (See Chapter 7 on selecting trees) Central California is a Mediterranean climate area. Mediterranean climate trees have adapted to growing and thriving in areas where the winters are mildly cold with rain, and the summers are hot and dry. They have mechanisms for standing up to the dry air, and of slowing, or stopping, the transpiration that would otherwise suck too much water out of their system. Some examples of Mediterranean climate trees are native California Oaks, Olive, Cork Oak, Italian Stone Pine, Grecian Laurel, and Italian Cypress. (Fig. 6-6, 6-7, 6-8, 6-9)

Why it matters:

Trees that have evolved in such places are not good at defending themselves from some of the pathogenic fungi that exist in the soil and multiply when conditions are moist and warm. This is because, in their normal situation, it is rarely warm and moist at the same time. Conditions would be cold when it's wet and dry when it's hot. The reason all of this matters to us is that we plant Mediterranean climate trees in our landscapes, often with the idea of having a tree suited to our climate, and then water the landscape thoroughly to keep all the

Fig. 6-6: An Interior Live Oak in the Central Valley foothills.

Fig. 6-7: Left to itself, this native Valley Oak does just fine.

Fig. 6-8: A Blue Oak showing off its ability to adapt to our sometimes tough climate and inhospitable locations.

Fig. 6-9: An Olive tree thrives in hot, dry summer environments.

other non-Mediterranean climate plants alive. We thus create a warm and wet soil condition in the summer. Soil-borne pathogenic fungi can then multiply and become strong enough to overpower the defenses of the tree that was never designed to withstand their onslaught in the first place. The tree then becomes infected with root rot diseases like Oak root rot or xylem-clogging diseases like Verticillium wilt. It is not that the tree doesn't like the water. It greatly appreciates it. Who wouldn't? It's hot! The problem is, the fungi appreciate it even more.

What you can do about it:
The best thing for these types of trees is to plant them in a space that can be maintained in a more-or-less native, summer dry, condition. Other small plants that can manage in a summer dry condition can be planted underneath or around such trees, so the landscape doesn't need to appear barren. These trees can be watered in summer, but carefully. They should be deep watered in one area under their canopy, then let that area dry out thoroughly before applying any more water. The areas watered can be staggered through the summer, never letting one area stay moist for an extended period. It is imperative with Mediterranean climate trees not to let the sprinklers actually throw water against the trunk of the tree for extended periods. (see Chapter 2 — "Crown Rot") The other option, if you can't reduce the irrigation to the desired location, is to plant a tree that has similar attributes as the Mediterranean climate tree you want, but make sure it can stand heat and high soil moisture. Substituting a Southern Live Oak for a Coast Live Oak would be a good example of substitution.

CHAPTER 7

PAPE'S TREE PICKS FOR THE CENTRAL VALLEY

A word about choosing trees: To choose a new tree for your landscape you have to consider several factors. First, will it tolerate our climate and the specific conditions where it will live? For instance, what sun exposure will it have, what irrigation quantity and quality, and what soil type? Next, what are your practical needs? Are you trying to shade something, maintain a view, create a screen, avoid overhead wires, plant by a pool, or avoid septic or sewer lines? Then consider your aesthetic objectives. Do you desire fall color, spring or summer bloom, multi-trunk or standard. By the time you sort through all of those criteria you will have come up with a list of a few trees that may suit your purposes and your circumstances.

The next step is to take a look at those candidates in a mature form somewhere, hopefully in your region. College campuses are often ideal for this. Some other options are other school campuses, botanical gardens, parks, and city streets. Of course, if you can locate a mature specimen at a friend or neighbor's house so much the better. Make sure to examine the root system of several individual trees. Examine the litter and the fall color, if any. This may mean that you need to actually consider the hunt for just the right tree to be a yearlong project. How else will you know what kind of litter issues it really has? If you locate the mature tree at a friend or neighbor's you can ask them for their experience with a specific tree, or you can always ask a professional in the tree industry. I believe it is best for you to see what that tree has to offer, both positive and negative, for yourself.

Once, you have chosen a tree you like, the key to helping it survive is to understand its needs as clearly as you can. The best way to do that is to find out what part of the world it is originally from, and what specific conditions you would find it in there. For example, the White Alder, *Alnus rhombifolia*, is native to California. That fact is not enough to really tell you about the tree's needs. If that was all you knew, you might think it would be able to stand up to full blazing sun and low water conditions in the summer. Once you discover that it is typically found in streambeds in foothill areas where water runs all year long with dozens, if not hundreds of its kind surrounding it, you can more clearly grasp this species' needs. This tree requires shade on its trunk, large amounts of available water, and prefers to be in an area where cool air moves through at night.

To keep a tree happy in its new environment you either need to match the tree to the specific environment you have or manipulate your environment to match its needs.

Central California is what is known as an interior Mediterranean climate. There are four other areas in the world that have a similar climate. They include a section of Chile, part of Australia, part of South Africa, and of course, the Mediterranean. Trees and plants from these areas are more likely to do well in our part of the world. An important thing to remember about this is that we change the environment around our houses and businesses from what would be natural, creating microclimates and especially changes in moisture availability. This is important when planting certain trees from Mediterranean climate areas. (See Chapter 6 — "Using Mediterranean Climate Trees") By changing the environment around us to some small extent, we can then more easily grow other trees and shrubs that otherwise would suffer greatly or not survive in our climate.

The trees described on the following pages are, of course, only a small portion of the options available. There are hundreds of trees that will grow in the Central Valley. They all have their place, but many have limited use in our area because of our unique conditions, aridity, soil and temperatures. The trees on the following list are trees that I feel particularly inclined to discuss, because of their usefulness or popularity.

LARGE-CROWNED DECIDUOUS SHADE TREES

Acer 'Autumn Fantasy' — Autumn Fantasy Maple

This tree is a cross between the Red Maple and the Silver Maple, both of which have more draw-backs than this offspring. It seems to have gotten the better traits of both parents. It grows faster than a Red Maple, but not so blazingly fast as a Silver Maple. This means that it has sturdier wood and less aggressive surface roots. Its leaves are light green on the top and sil-very underneath. It has better fall color than either of its parents. In fall the tops of the leaves are a brilliant red and the undersides are hot magenta. It needs plenty of water in our environment and should probably have its bark protected from the hot sun on the southwest side until it is old enough to shade itself. (See Chapter 3 — "Sunscalding") Grows to 60 feet tall and 40 feet wide. (Fig. 7-1)

Celtis sinensis — Chinese Hackberry

This tree has the classic umbrella shape, moderate to fast growth, and dark green, shiny, attractively-toothed leaves. When it matures it has a uniquely ridged trunk, somewhat like that of a mature olive tree. It looks much like a Chinese Elm in overall shape, but usually has a much less aggressive root system than the elm. The one real drawback to this tree is that in recent years in our area it has been overtaken by a wooly aphid, which

Fig. 7-1: Autumn Fantasy Maple

Fig. 7-2: Chinese Hackberry

Fig. 7-3: Fruitless Mulberry

finally arrived here from China. This insect can make a huge mess of the tree and everything under it, creating a drippy coating, as if the tree had been sprayed with maple syrup. If you choose to have this tree you would need to treat it once every year with a systemic insecticide such as imidacloprid (Merit/Bayer systemic — See Chapter 5 — "Sucking Insects") until such time as beneficial predatory or parasitic insects begin controlling its populations. The fall color of Chinese hackberry is nothing special. Its fruit is small and hard, not messy. Grows to 40 feet tall and about the same wide. It is a great overall shade tree. (Fig. 7-2)

Morus alba 'Fruitless' — Fruitless Mulberry

This is one of the all time best trees for shade. Oh no, you say. Oh yes, I say. It has huge dark green leaves in a dense canopy. This tree has gotten a bad reputation, which is only partially deserved. If it is pruned correctly as it matures, planted in the appropriate location and deep watered, it can be one of the best for keeping the hot Central Valley sun at bay. It seems that many people believe they must trim this tree back to the main scaffold branches every winter. That is a ludicrous idea. I believe that idea came about because of the experience people had with the fruiting mulberry. Fruiting mulberries have an enormous amount of sweet, sticky fruit that creates a huge mess under the tree. No individual family could make enough mulberry pie to rid themselves of the mess. People recognized that the tree only fruits on wood that is a year or more old. If they cut off all of last year's growth every year during the winter, then the following season there would be no fruit. After years of this kind of treatment based on keeping the fruit off, people translated that pruning style to fruitless mulberries as well, even though, there was no basis for it. When a tree is pruned in that harsh fashion for many years, it creates a lot of work that is expensive and resented, because of fast growing, long, ratty-looking secondary branches. The tree becomes ugly with large decaying and weak scaffold branches, thus the bad reputation. If pruned correctly, fruitless mulberries can be a moderate to fast growing tree to 35 to 50 feet high and wide, where they slow to a manageable size. After years of appropriate pruning, a mulberry maintains a branching structure as beautiful as any other tree. Its true drawback is its aggressive root system. It definitely needs room where it grows. Do not plant it near fences, walkways, or pools. When this tree reaches maturity it will be too shady and there will be too much root competition to grow turf under it. If a tough tree with serious shade is more important to you than lawn to mow, a fruitless mulberry will do the job. (Fig. 7-3)

> *Tree at my window,*
> *window tree, My sash is*
> *lowered when night comes on;*
> *But let there never be curtain*
> *drawn between you and me.*
>
> — Robert Frost

Fig. 7-4: Chinese Pistache

Pistacia chinensis — Chinese Pistache

This tree is a reliable, moderate sized tree of about 35 to 40 feet high by as wide. Its growth is slow to moderate. It is lanky and a bit skimpy looking when young, but when it matures it is a nicely rounded, full shade tree. It has excellent fall color ranging from yellow and gold through orange and red, to a deep burgundy, often more than one color per tree, and sometimes almost all one color on a tree. There is a variety called 'Keith Davey', which is a male grafted variety. It has no fruit and a consistent deep red color. The female pistache trees have a small fruit that is usually not messy, but if the tree has a huge crop, maintenance can be problematic to some people. The roots of a Chinese Pistache are usually tame

Fig. 7-5: Chinese Pistache in fall color

Fig. 7-6: Chinese Pistache fruit and foliage

Fig. 7-7: Valley Oak

and it can be planted in tight planters, down to about 6 feet wide. (Fig. 7-4, 7-5, 7-6)

Quercus lobata — Valley Oak

This tree is native to the Central Valley of California and the surrounding foothills. It is a moderate grower. Its leaves have the classic, lobed, oak leaf shape. It is one of the most majestic trees you can have in your landscape. It can reach 75 feet high. Valley Oaks typically get quite a few interesting galls on the back of their leaves. The galls are caused by a minute wasp. The galls don't do a significant amount of damage to the tree. Through much of the year, these trees drop something such as catkins, acorns, leaves, and galls. Although Valley Oaks grow faster with some extra water, once established, they can survive summers without any extra water, making them ideal for water conserving landscapes. (Fig. 7-7)

LARGE-CROWNED EVERGREEN TREES

Cinnamomum camphora — Camphor

This is one of the largest broad-leaved evergreen trees that grow in our area. It can be truly majestic when mature. It has light green leaves that come out with a slight coppery tinge when new. It has a beautiful branching structure with green bark when young, changing to a rugged gray and black with age. The fruit is small, hard, and mostly inconsequential. Because its bark is tender when young, it should be protected from the direct southwest sun until it can shade itself. This tree has a unique medicinal smell that some folks enjoy and others revile. It will grow to approximately 50 feet tall and as wide. There are two main problems with Camphor trees. It seems as if something is falling nearly year-round. It drops leaves, flowers, seeds, flower stalks, and small stems at various times. The other issue is its aggressive root system. This tree needs room both for its canopy and its root system. Don't plant it close to landscape infrastructure or buildings. (Fig. 7-8, 7-9)

Fig. 7-8: Camphor

Fig. 7-9: Camphor foliage and bark

Our ordinary mind always tries to persuade us that we are nothing but acorns and that our greatest happiness will be to become bigger, fatter, shinier acorns; but that is of interest only to pigs. Our faith gives us knowledge of something better: that we can become oak trees.

— E.F. Schumacher

Pinus pinea —
Italian Stone Pine

Most people think of pine trees as growing in a conical "Christmas tree" shape. This pine breaks out of that mold. It is an extremely round-headed tree. This tree has long, dark green needles and brown, fissured bark. When young, it is like a huge green globe near the ground. As it matures, that globe of foliage can rise to nearly 80 feet on very large upright scaffold branches. It is a Mediterranean-climate tree and can easily take the heat and low water of our summer climate. Because of its size it requires sufficient room both above and below to do its stuff. Its main mess is, like any other pine tree, a blanket of needles building beneath it. Its seeds are edible. (Fig. 7-10)

Quercus agrifolia —
Coast Live Oak

A California native tree, this oak is a moderate grower with majestic proportions when mature. It can grow 50 to 70 feet tall and even wider. It has small oval, cupped, and somewhat prickly leaves. There is much variation in the leaves between trees and even on the same tree. Some will be more cupped, or more toothed, or smooth, or rounded than others. Like most oaks, it drops some amount of catkins, leaves, acorns and other parts throughout the

Fig. 7-10: Italian Stone Pine

year. Its roots are sometimes tame and at other times quite obnoxious, depending on soil and other growing conditions. This is the classic Central California foothill oak of the coast range and inland around Southern California. Its bark is gray, smooth when young, and fissured as it ages. As with the other large trees, give it space. Be careful not to over water during summer, especially close to the root crown. (See Chapter 6 — "Using Mediterranean Climate Trees") (Fig. 7-11, 7-12)

Quercus suber — Cork Oak

This is a unique tree that appreciates our climate here in the Central Valley. It is one of the more interesting oak trees. It has the corkiest bark of all corky barks. This is the tree that cork for wine bottles comes from. The cork gives its trunk a unique look. The leaves of the cork oak are grayer than its California native cousins, so it is a striking tree in the landscape. When it is mature it has pendulous outer branches that really make it stand out. It is from the Mediterranean, so we must be careful where in the landscape we place it, so that it doesn't get too much irrigation. (See Chapter 6 — "Using Mediterranean Climate Trees") As with other oaks it

Fig. 7-11: Coast Live Oak

Fig. 7-12: Coast Live Oak

Fig. 7-13: Cork Oak

Fig. 7-14: Cork Oak bark

drops components regularly. Although it is evergreen, it tends to drop most of its leaves in the early spring. Its roots are tame. Cork Oak grows to 50 feet high and wide. (Fig. 7-13, 7-14)

Quercus virginiana — Southern Live Oak

This oak tree is from a part of the country, the southeast, that has plenty of summer water. If you want a large evergreen oak that can tolerate lots of garden water in

Fig. 7-15: Southern Live Oak

the landscape, as opposed to its Mediterranean cousins mentioned above, this is the one for you. The one cautionary thing to remember is its very aggressive root system. This tree can take over a large area with its surface roots, especially in soil conditions common to the Central Valley. It is a beautiful dark green, becomes very broad (approximately 50 feet high by 80 feet wide in our climate), and is quite shady. Make sure you have the room for this tree before planting. The gall that frequently lives on this tree is worth mentioning. It is a small bit of tan fuzz about three-eighths of an inch across on the backside of the leaves. It can be a bit annoying when mass quantities of it fall into your landscape, but otherwise it is relatively harmless. (Fig. 7-15)

UPRIGHT DECIDUOUS TREES

Ginkgo biloba —
Ginkgo or Maidenhair Tree

This relic of a prehistoric era is one of the best behaved, most interesting trees you can put in your landscape. The ginkgo is the sole living link between the lower and higher plants, between ferns and conifers. Its one real drawback is the slowness of its growth. It can take 10 to 12 years to reach 20 feet. It usually grows very upright in its youth, then broadens out somewhat in maturity (sounds familiar doesn't it). A ginkgo can reach 70 to 80 feet if very old. The usual mature height in the Central Valley is 40 to 50 feet.

Ginkgos tolerate a broad range of soil and water conditions and have tame roots. The bark is a light gray, nearly white with small darker fissures, and very attractive. Most ginkgos have a radiant golden fall color. It is especially beau-

tiful if you leave the golden carpet of leaves on the ground for a while as the tree goes dormant, creating a colorfully magical place out of your landscape. The leaves are a unique triangular shape with a pronounced flow to the veining.

Fig. 7-16: Ginkgo leaves

Fig. 7-17: Ginkgo

> Trees are poems that
> earth writes upon the sky,
> We fell them down and
> turn them into paper,
> That we may record
> our emptiness.
>
> — Kahlil Gibran

Fig. 7-18: Tupelo

Fig. 7-19: Tupelo leaves

Make sure you get a grafted male variety. Ginkgos from seed are typically just as good looking, but if you get a female tree, it will eventually drop great quantities of fruit that smell just like dog poop. It can really take the fun out of a barbecue or game of catch in the backyard. (7-16, 7-17)

Nyssa sylvatica — Tupelo or Sour Gum

This is a relatively new tree to our area. Tupelo is a tree that comes from the eastern U.S. It is prized mainly for its fiery reddish-orange glowing fall color. It grows somewhat conical when young, and gets a little rough around the

Fig. 7-20: Red Oak

Fig. 7-21: Scarlet Oak leaves

edges when older. They grow to 40 feet tall by 20 feet wide. Tupelos do best with significant summer water, as you would expect from an eastern tree. The female trees have a small dark fruit that doesn't make much of a mess. (Fig. 7-18, 7-19)

Quercus rubra or *coccinea* — Red or Scarlet Oak

These two oak trees and some other eastern U.S. oaks tend to have an upright, conical shape when younger, much like the trees mentioned above. They typically have deep roots. The leaves are the classic, lobed, oak shape with points on the lobes. They turn dramatic reds and oranges in the fall. Because these are eastern trees they need some consistent summer moisture and fairly fertile soil. They can reach a height of 60 to 80 feet, have gray bark and can produce an occasionally heavy crop of acorns. (Fig. 7-20, 7-21)

> *Evolution did not intend trees to grow singly. Far more than ourselves they are social creatures, and no more natural as isolated specimens than man is as a marooned sailor or hermit.*
>
> — John Fowles

UPRIGHT EVERGREEN TREES

Cedrus atlantica 'Glauca' — Blue Atlas Cedar

This tree has the classic Christmas tree shape and a wonderful blue color to the leaves. It can approach 60 feet tall, but takes its time. When healthy and happy, this is one of the most striking trees in the landscape, mainly due to its color and texture. The needles are approximately one inch long. The biggest problem with this tree in the Central Valley is that sapsuckers love to drill holes in its bark. So much so that it can be destroyed by the constant stress of loosing so much sap once it becomes rid-

Fig. 7-22: Blue Atlas Cedar

Fig. 7-23: Blue Atlas Cedar foliage

dled with holes. The best way to protect against woodpeckers is to cover the trunk by winding it with plastic netting like you would use to keep birds off your fruit trees near harvest time. Most of the litter of this tree falls straight below the canopy and creates a thick duff that typically inhibits the growth of any other plant material below it. (Fig. 7-22, 7-23)

Fig. 7-24: Deodar Cedar

Cedrus deodara — Deodar Cedar

This tree is similar to the Blue Atlas Cedar, except its color is typically a soft green-gray. This species also weeps more than its blue cousin. It comes from the Himalaya, so it can tolerate a broad range of harsh conditions (perfect for the Central Valley). Make sure not to get continuous water against the base of this tree. It is very susceptible to crown rot. (See Chapter 2) It also can succumb to the constant pestering of sapsuckers. This tree is often used as a large Christmas tree and needs plenty of space. It can reach 80 feet in height and 60 feet wide. There are many variations amongst individual trees in this species. Some look grayer than others, some more light green. Some are more bushy and thick while others are spindly. These trees also suffer from spontaneous limb drop (See Chapter 6). Be certain your Deodar Cedar is not over thinned by an unaware tree trimmer. Such pruning can cause the bark to burn, which in turn causes many other problems. The litter of this tree is the same as mentioned above with the Blue Atlas Cedar. (Fig. 7-24)

Pinus canariensis —
Canary Island Pine

This tree was once so popular in California that you couldn't find one in a nursery that wasn't tagged by a landscape architect holding it for use at some future time. Recently, they have fallen out of favor, mainly because of the difficult to control litter caused by the very long, triple needle bunches that get hung up in smaller understory plants. This tree is still useful if you need an evergreen tree that goes straight up and you can manage the needle litter beneath it. It is a dark green and makes quite a statement against the blue sky because of its tiered silhouette. It grows relatively fast to 60 to 80 feet. This tree needs almost no trimming, except the occasional dead limb. It also has the helpful quality, that if a limb does break, unlike the deodar cedar, it will typically hang in the tree until you retrieve it. Another aspect that people consider a drawback to Canary Island Pines, like other pines, is the huge amount of pollen that they can produce during the spring. This large production of pollen is not so much a problem for allergy prone people, as it is a huge mess producer. However, the pollen can be washed away very easily. This tree

Fig. 7-25: Canary Island Pine

tolerates a broad range of conditions, and even when it turns brown in a severe freeze, will revive once the weather warms. (Fig. 7-25)

Sequoia sempervirens
'Aptos Blue' or 'Soquel' —
Coastal Redwood

This is probably the most popular tree in the Central Valley. It is a beautiful constant green, as well mannered as any tree when it comes to mess, and creates a great screen. The problem is that it was designed to live at the coast of California not in an inland valley. (See Chapter 6) When it is not damaged by the harsher, dryer conditions of the Central Valley, it can be used to positive effect. One point people often forget concerning sequoias, as well as with trees in general, is how tall and wide they will eventually become. Because this tree is relatively new in its popularity, in regard to tree planting trends, the full scale of its presence hasn't been obvious to everyone. On the coast, where it is native, it has become one of the two biggest trees in the world, along with its distant cousin in the mountains, the giant redwood. Coastal Redwoods drop their litter nearly straight down below the canopy, creating a thick duff in the deep shade of the canopy. This fact, along with their very competitive roots makes it nearly impossible to grow anything beneath them. The Aptos Blue variety is a darker green with slightly more horizontal branching. The Soquel variety is a lighter green with more upright branching and is typically sparser between branches. There are other varieties of Coastal Redwood, but these are the two standout varieties, and they are the most easily available.

Coastal Redwoods can reach over 300 feet in their native forest. They typically can reach 50 to 70 feet in the Central Valley and up to 30 feet wide. (Fig. 7-26)

Fig. 7-26: Coastal Redwood

There is always music amongst the trees in the garden, but our hearts must be very quiet to hear it.

— Minnie Aumonier

SMALL FLOWERING DECIDUOUS TREES

The following trees are probably some of the best trees to plant in your yard if you are trying to avoid visits from the public utility tree contractor. Public utilities are required by law to keep trees trimmed well away from the power lines. When the contracted trimmer prunes a tree it is done only to remove those limbs that are near the lines. There is no attempt to trim to any aesthetic standard.

Cercis occidentalis or 'Oklahoma' — Redbud

This is one of the toughest flowering trees you can put in your garden. The Western Redbud, *Cercis occidentalis*, grows vigorously in the foothills of the Sierra Nevada surrounding the Central Valley, with no summer water and no relief from summer heat. It should not receive water against the trunk, although it will grow a little better if it receives a small amount of supplemental water during the summer. *Cercis* 'Oklahoma' is slightly friendlier to normal garden water. Both trees are covered with bright pink to magenta flower buds first thing in the spring before many leaves are showing. This is one of the more spectacular flowering garden trees when in bloom. I prefer, and think the genus prefers, a multi-trunk form. The seedpods, which eventually look like rust colored pea pods can persist on the tree all the way through to the next year. Some folks are not fond of them. Personally, I think they add to the seasonal colors of the garden in an attractive way. The leaves of redbuds are a unique rounded shape, rare among commonly available trees. Redbuds can reach 15 to 20 feet in height and width. (Fig. 7-27, 7-28)

Fig. 7-27: Redbud

Fig. 7-28: Redbud flowers

Fig. 7-29: Desert Willow

Fig. 7-30: Desert Willow flowers

Fig. 7-31: Chinese Fringe Tree

Chilopsis linearis — Desert Willow

This tree is native to the Southwestern United States & Mexico. Like the redbud, it can handle severe conditions, including poor soil and high winds. It has a thin willow-like leaf, thus the name. Its branches are upright, so in that sense it does not weep like a willow, but its leaves hang in a slightly willowy way. It grows fast to 15 to 20 feet, and then slows. It has gorgeous pink and white trumpet-shaped flowers that bloom from spring through the warm season. There are several varieties with more striking, darker colors ranging from burgundy to purple and in combinations. The one drawback of this plant is its long, thin, bean-like seedpods that cover the tree through to the next year. They eventually turn gray and can make the tree look a bit unkempt. (Fig. 7-29, 7-30)

Fig. 7-32: Chinese Fringe Tree flowers

Chionanthus retusus — Chinese Fringe Tree

This is a somewhat rare tree in the Central Valley, but it is available. It has a most wonderful late spring blossom show. The flowers look like pure white bundles of fringe. The seeds are a small black fruit about the size of a pea and typically do not cause too much of a mess. In my opinion, whatever seed mess comes from this tree is a small price to pay for the great flower display. The leaves are round and dark green. The bark is interesting. Its coloration is a mix of greenish-yellow and tan when young to brown and gray when older. It has a unique, somewhat papery flakiness to it. This tree only grows to about 20 feet and doesn't get there in a hurry. (Fig. 7-31, 7-32)

Cotinus coggygria — Smoke Tree

Smoke Tree is another great tree for the Central Valley because it tolerates such a broad range of conditions. I have seen this tree planted in the most inhospitable, poor soil and low water areas, and it still looks respectable, although it will grow slower under such circumstances. It may actually look better when grown under what would be considered poor condi-

tions. This is one of those plants that thrives on neglect. It has very round leaves. Some varieties have

Fig. 7-33: Smoke Tree foliage

Fig. 7-34: Smoke Tree flower

Fig. 7-35: Smoke Tree

Fig. 7-36: Crape Myrtle with flowers

Fig. 7-37: Crape Myrtle in fall color

Fig. 7-38: Crape Myrtle

bronze to purple leaves. Some of those varieties keep that color all year while others fade gently to green during the summer. These purple varieties also have the best flower show, which is not like your standard flower show. It got its name because the flowers come out on fine stems, and as they fade they send out extremely fine pinkish fuzz that from a distance looks like a haze of smoke around the plant. This tree is smallish, 15 to 20 feet tall, and is best used as a multi-trunk tree. To top it off, the fall color of a smoke tree can be absolutely fiery and glowing. (Fig. 7-33, 7-34, 7-35)

Lagerstroemia indica — Crape Myrtle

Here is a tree with both a solid history of use and a multitude of positive attributes. It is a slow tree, ideal for small, tight planters. Its roots will not usually cause any problems. My favorite feature about Crape Myrtle is the bark. It is like a jigsaw puzzle of very subtle colors. I actually think this tree, especially if carefully pruned, is more attractive with its leaves off. Crape Myrtles are reliable summer bloomers no matter how you prune them because they flower on this year's growth. They come in a multitude of colors including white, pink, hot pink, watermelon, salmon, lavender, purple, peppermint, brick red, and true red. They thrive in hot conditions. The problems with Crape Myrtles are aphids (which are easy to treat), basal suckering, and powdery mildew. Crape Myrtle varieties with names of North American Indian tribes are hybrids that are more resistant to powdery mildew. Some of these Indian tribe varieties also grow somewhat bigger and faster than the straight *indica* varieties, and some have a warm cinnamon color to the bark. This tree is fine in either a standard tree form or a multi-trunk form. Crape Myrtles can grow from 5 to 25 feet depending on the variety. (Fig. 7-36, 7-37, 7-38)

Malus sp. — Flowering Crabapple

Flowering crabapples have been around a long time and there are scores of varieties. Many of the older varieties have a multitude of insect and disease problems. I suggest if you are interested in crabapples, investigate some of the newer, more disease resistant varieties. My personal preference is 'Prairie Fire.' The great thing about Flowering Crabapples are the combinations of spring leaf color, flower color, summer leaf

color, fruit size and color, and fall color that they come in. The leaves can vary throughout the year from purple to bronze to pink to light green and dark green. The flowers can be white, pink, dark pink, white and pink, red, you get the idea. The fruit can be very small to moderate and comes in green, pink, red, wine, yellow, and

Fig. 7-39: Flowering Crabapple

Fig. 7-40: Flowering Crabapple flowers

can be quite ornamental, if a bit messy. This is probably not a tree to plant over a walkway or parking spot. It can get scale, aphids and fire blight among other things. Good cultural practices can reduce the chances of such problems. Typical size varies from 15 to 20 feet in height and width. (Fig. 7-39, 7-40)

Fig. 7-41: Evergreen Pear

Fig. 7-42: Evergreen Pear

Pyrus kawakami — Evergreen Pear

This is the old standby flowering pear tree that for some time fell out of favor because other flowering pears came into vogue. In my opinion, the only thing truly problematic about this tree is its susceptibility to fire blight. This problem is small if the tree is sprayed preventatively to reduce the risk of the disease or acted on quickly once the disease is evident. Evergreen pears are not truly evergreen, at least not in the Central Valley, and thank goodness, because the fall color is fantastic. It is a mix of red, purple, orange, gold and green that is stunning, collectively on the tree and even on individual leaves. It has beautiful white flowers in the early spring. It is one of the earliest to bloom, usually in February, and blooms before many of its leaves have unfurled. This pear has a very rough, very dark, checkered bark that is attractive, especially after a rain, against the backdrop of the fallen white flowers. It has fruit that can be a mess, but is much

Fig. 7-43: Evergreen Pear flowers

less messy than the other commonly used flowering pears such as Bradford Pear and Aristocrat Pear (extremely messy). One of the best attributes of this tree is its broad shape, often wider than it is tall. This tree grows about 25 feet tall and as wide. With appropriate pruning it can become quite a stately tree. (Fig. 7-41, 7-42, 7-43)

Vitex agnus-castus — Chaste Tree

If you want a fast growing, summer flowering, smallish tree, this one might be for you. It is a bit lanky and suckery when young, but if given a yearly pruning to realign it to your needs and control its suckers, it can become elegant and interesting. It grows fast to about 15 to 20 feet. The commonly available varieties have dark green leaves with a bit of gray, and blue to purple flowers in the summer from June until October. The resultant seeds are small, about the size of a peppercorn, and crunchy. They don't make too much of a mess, but can sprout where they end up if conditions are right. The Chaste Trees grown from seed tend to have a slightly smaller, grayer leaf and the flowers run from a pinkish creamy white to lavender and purple. You never know which it will be. The biggest

Fig. 7-44: Chaste Tree

drawback to this tree is its greedy root system. The roots typically don't get big enough to cause serious infrastructure damage, but can suck up all the water and nutrients in a planter, especially near the surface. If you want to have a tree that grows like a Japanese Maple, but can take the Central Valley heat, even on a western or southern exposure, this is it. It even has palmate leaves like a Japanese Maple, and as a bonus it flowers. It is great in a multi-trunk or low branching form. Its trunk and scaffold branches become gnarly and shaggy, appearing somewhat like a miniature mature Oak. (Fig. 7-44)

SMALL EVERGREEN TREES

Unfortunately, there are not a lot of great small evergreen trees for our Central Valley landscapes. As mentioned in the prior category of trees, these trees are good for planting under power lines.

Arbutus unedo or A. 'Marina' — Strawberry Tree

This is one of my favorite trees. The bark of this tree is a rich red to cinnamon brown (somewhat like a manzanita), with hints of green and gold where the bark is peeling off. The bark, before it peels, is rough but once it has shed has a tactile-pleasing smoothness. Because this tree (especially the straight *unedo* species) grows so

Fig. 7-45: 'Marina' Strawberry Tree

slowly, it results in an intriguing, twisting, turning, branching structure that bears admiring. It can reach 25 to 40 feet depending on conditions. The leaves are a dark green and slightly toothed. The flowers are white, tinged with pink, and gracefully shaped like upside down urns. The fruit begins as a hard green ball, can change to yellow and orange, but ends up as a bright red rough-skinned ball about the size of a cherry. It is edible, but is a bit mealy. It has one serious problem — it is messy. This tree should never be planted over a walkway. It should always be put where the fruit can fall into a thick ground-cover or some place where it will not be a problem. It can get scale and aphids (See Chapter 5 — "Sucking Insects"), but any good gardener should be able to handle those common pests (I suggest a systemic treatment only after sign of pest infestation). The 'Marina' variety of this genus is an excellent choice. It grows somewhat faster

Fig. 7-46: Strawberry Tree fruit and flowers

than *unedo*, and its leaves are substantially larger. The 'Marina' makes a better standard tree form, while the *unedo* makes a better multi or low branching form. (Fig. 7-45, 7-46)

Laurus nobilis —
Grecian Laurel or Sweet Bay
Here is a truly classic tree. This is a Mediterranean climate tree actually from the Mediterranean. It is the "noble" tree whose leaves and branches were used to create the laurel wreaths placed upon the heads of those honored in early Greek and Roman history. So, don't sit back on your laurels, plant one! It is also the bay leaf used in your mom's spaghetti sauce. This tree can grow to about 30 feet tall or more, but grows slowly. It makes a nice screening shrub or tree. It can be sheered to create formal garden shapes or be kept to a specific size. Its leaves are a pleasant dark green, with a hint of gray on the underside and somewhat leathery. When crushed they

> *Character is like a tree and reputation like a shadow. The shadow is what we think of it; the tree is the real thing.*
> — Abraham Lincoln

give off a pleasant sweet, spicy smell. The flowers are attractive, yellow and white, but not that noticeable when present. The fruit is round, dark purple, about 3/4" diameter and can be messy over walkways. Bay trees are susceptible to scale and can be treated systemically once the infestation appears. (See Chapter 5 — "Sucking Insects") (Fig. 7-47, 7-48)

Fig. 7-47: Bay Laurel foliage

Fig. 7-48: Bay Laurel

PALMS

There are many varieties of palms that I could write about. However, I would like to mention the ones I feel are most interesting and appropriate for our climate. The climatic factor that most limits palms in our area is the winter cold. Many palms are tropical or subtropical, and inclined to grow in areas of the world where cold winters do not occur, so they haven't developed a tolerance for low temperatures. The palms on my list are tolerant of the level of cold encountered in the Central Valley. Remember, when it comes to palms, the most popular or most available ones, aren't necessarily the best ones.

Fig. 7-49: Mexican Blue Palm

Brahea armata — Mexican Blue Palm

If you like fan palms, but are bored by the very common, and often inappropriately used Mexican and California Fan Palms, genus *Washingtonia*, try this more unusual tree. It has strikingly silvery blue leaves. The flowers are actually quite showy, weeping cream colored plumes. This is one tough tree, tolerating high temperatures, high winds and low temperatures to about 18° F. It is a very stately looking tree that grows slow enough to keep it out of much trouble. Grows slowly to 20 to 40 feet tall. (Fig. 7-49)

Brahea edulis — Guadalupe Palm

This tree looks similar to a green version of its cousin mentioned above or a *Washingtonia*. Unlike *Brahea armata*, this tree's fronds are green, and unlike the *Washingtonias*, the frond and the frond bases fall away easily once they dry up, leaving a clean trunk.

If trees could scream, would we be so cavalier about cutting them down? We might, if they screamed all the time, for no good reason.

— Jack Handey

In my book, this palm is much more attractive and easier to maintain than the *Washingtonias*, and because it grows very slowly, is easier to control. Both these *Brahea* species are very tough trees. The species name *edulis* refers to the fact that the fruit is edible. Grows slowly to 30 feet. (Fig. 7-50)

Butia capitata — Pindo Palm

This is my favorite palm for the Central Valley. It has a very stately feather frond, with gray-green coloring. In my opinion, the clean lines and tidy, recurving fronds of this tree are far more attractive than the disheveled looking fronds of the more popular Queen Palm. This tree is very tolerant of cold conditions, and grows quite slowly to 20 feet. An established tree can survive temperatures down to 12°F. When the old fronds have been pruned off, it creates an interesting pattern on the trunk. The flowers are not as messy as some palms. The fruit is an orange color and edible. (Fig. 7-51)

Chamaerops humilis — Mediterranean Fan Palm

This palm is a common tree in most of California, and for good reason. It is a tough, beautiful, naturally multi-trunk tree.

Mediterranean Fan Palms are often used as large focal point plantings around commercial buildings. The maintenance is reasonable, and they tolerate a large range of conditions. This tree can actually survive for short periods at temperatures nearing 0°F. Some individual plants have bright green leaves, while others

Fig. 7-50: Guadalupe Palm

Fig. 7-51: Pindo Palm

will have gray-green leaves. The only real drawback to this tree is, if you have to trim it, you will undoubtedly encounter its small, but innumerable and prickly spines. Make sure this palm is placed where it has room to spread because it can often reach 20 feet wide and as high. (Fig. 7-52)

Fig. 7-52: Mediterranean Fan Palm

Trachycarpus fortunei — Windmill Palm

The windmill palm has a small fan leaf very similar to the Mediterranean fan palm. The two big differences are that this tree is a single trunk tree and has no spines on the petiole. It has small teeth along the leaf petiole that are not likely to poke you, making this an easier tree to trim. A unique characteristic of this tree is its hairy trunk. The trunk is covered with a course fiber. A very hardy tree, down to 10°F, it tolerates difficult conditions. Windmill palms typically can get to about 30 feet tall. (Fig. 7-53)

Fig. 7-53: Windmill Palm

> *If you don't like how things are, change it! You're not a tree.*
>
> — Jim Rohn

CHAPTER 8

PROCEED AT YOUR OWN RISK
Trees You Shouldn't Plant

Well, we've talked about everything else, now it's time to talk about the trees I recommend you avoid. Just as the trees we discussed in the last chapter are only a small portion of the trees that are available and worthy to be planted, the trees named here are not the only trees that can cause problems. Also, just as the trees in chapter seven are not good in all circumstances, the trees named here are not "bad" in all circumstances. What typically makes a tree a truly poor choice is either its aggressive behavior, or its lack of adaptibility to our area and your needs. They can have huge amounts of seed drop, which creates a mess or worse, a huge crop of seedlings where you don't want them (weeds). Aggressive surface roots or root suckers are the result of many an uninformed tree choice. Worst of all is the tree which is so beautiful that you can't resist it, but it takes constant and multiple kinds of care and worry, yet slowly dies over time, torturing its owner and wasting time and money. Well, let's get on with it. Read and be warned!

Ailanthus altissima — Tree-of-Heaven...or...
"Tree from Hell"

This is certainly the appropriate tree to start off a list of trees not to plant. The good news is you would likely never see this plant for sale in a reputable nursery. If you do, it's not really reputable. It is what is not so fondly referred to as a trash tree. This is one of those

Fig. 8-1: Tree-of-Heaven

Fig. 8-2: Tree-of-Heaven foliage

Fig. 8-3: Dogwood

trees that you may temporarily admire for its bold look, tough constitution and ease of propagation, but soon your admiration would turn to revulsion should you choose to plant it on your property, or even your neighbor's. It spreads quickly by root suckers and seeds. It grows quickly in any soil. It stinks, will take over your world should you turn your back, and it is difficult to get rid of. Did I say it stinks? The only reason to plant this tree is if absolutely nothing else will grow, in which case you should probably move anyway. (Fig. 8-1, 8-2)

Cornus florida — Eastern Dogwood...

"Burning Dollar Bills"

This is one of the more beautiful trees you could have growing in your yard. I can hear the protests already — "I have one of those in my yard and it does perfectly." Well, that may be the case for some, and when it does work, it is fantastic. The problem is, it rarely works. This tree is native to the eastern U.S. Its preference is for humid, wet summer heat with slightly acid, well-drained soil. What does it usually get when we plant it in the Central Valley? It gets arid, dry summer heat with slightly alkaline, poorly-drained soil. Nearly no nurseries in Central or Southern California actually grow these trees. The overwhelming majority of Eastern Dogwoods sold in California are grown in Oregon or Washington. Why? Even professional growers cannot get them to grow here with consistent success. Because of that fact and the fact that it is such a beautiful tree when it does work, this tree is typically much more expensive than other trees of the same size. You might have to plant five or ten of these trees, constantly changing the drainage, soil composition and exposure, before you get one to really establish itself in a California interior valley. If you have the dough to burn, give it a try. (Fig. 8-3)

Fraxinus angustifolia 'Raywoodii' — Raywood Ash...

"It was such a good tree when it was young, where did I go wrong?"

When this tree was introduced it looked like a tree with all the answers. It grew fairly fast, had a tidy growth habit, was not too big, had beautiful fall color, and had no seed drop. Man, what a great tree! — for a while. The problems with this tree begin when it starts to reach its adolescence. Raywood Ash trees usually have aggressive

surface root problems. The truth is they shouldn't really be blamed for this shortcoming. The real problem is in the rootstock growers have chosen to graft it onto. The "Raywood" part of the tree is as described above, and relatively tame. The rootstock is from some incredibly aggressive, earth swallowing, B-class sci-fi movie type of rootstock. It may possibly be from Shamel Ash (see below). These roots can be very destructive to sidewalks, driveways, fences, and foundations. Whatever the rootstock's origin, I do not understand why growers con-

Fig. 8-4: Raywood Ash

tinue to use it, when its drawbacks have become so evident. There may be some Raywood Ash on tamer rootstock, unfortunately if you cannot find out; it is not worth the risk. Another unfortunate problem afflicting Raywood Ash is a disease called Raywood Ash Dieback, thought to be caused by the botryosphaeria fungus (See Chapter 4 — "Branch Dieback"). This disease has become a serious threat to Raywoods. It can be treated by an application, preferably by intracambial injection, of a special high phosphorous, high potassium fertilizer. Better yet, choose a different tree. (Fig. 8.4)

Fig. 8-5: Shamel Ash

Fraxinus uhdei — Shamel Ash...

"Volcano of Wood"

This tree used to be quite popular in Southern California, but I have yet to understand why. Probably the kindest thing you can say about it is that it grows fast, if that's what you need. Planting one of these trees is somewhat like planting a leaf and wood volcano in your yard. It creates a giant cone around its base. It is very prone to surface roots and what's worse, the base of the trunk will hump up the soil around it to an amazing extent. The branching structure is such that the angle of attachment is very tight. From a maintenance point of view it is incredibly hard on your feet when climbing, and the limbs somewhat more prone to breakage. If you don't have a lot of space, this tree will surely be too big. Aphids are a regular pest on the tender outer leaves of Shamel Ash, raining down a fine mist of honeydew (See Chapter 5). In an urban/sub-

Fig. 8-6: Shamel Ash roots

urban environment this tree belongs on the "bad" list. (Fig. 8-5, 8-6)

Ligustrum lucidum — Glossy Leaf Privet...

"Does Not Believe in Birth Control"

This is a tree, that under certain specific circumstances, could actually be admired. It is tough, it does not get too large, and it is evergreen. This tree has become a weed tree throughout much of the Central Valley. Once it reaches maturity it has massive amounts of small staining fruit that come on after what some folks consider foul smelling flowers. The flower odor, even if considered pleasant or tolerable, can be quite strong. That is just the start of the troubles. Once the seeds hit the ground they can become a thick weed patch of baby privets for you to keep after. On top of that, the birds, who retrieve many of the seeds before they fall, even from your neighbor's tree down the road, will kindly deposit them all

Fig. 8-8: Glossy Leaf Privet flowers

Fig. 8-7: Glossy Leaf Privet

over your yard where they will assuredly sprout to become an unwanted volunteer with tough roots. This tree is often seen growing up through your desirable shrubs and trees, unnoticed until it is large enough to be difficult to remove without damaging the surrounding vegetation. It can be kept nice if thinned regularly, but creates more work than most people want to do. If you like to work constantly, then I recommend it. (Fig. 8-7, 8-8)

Fig. 8-9: Aristocrat Pear flowers

Fig. 8-10: Aristocrat Pear

Pyrus calleryana 'Aristocrat' — Aristocrat Flowering Pear...
"Problem Ridden"

This tree started out to be the new improved flowering pear variety with a more upright growth pattern and super white flowers. The problem is it turned out to be a troubled tree in the Central Valley. It is much more susceptible to fire blight (See Chapter 5) than the two other commonly planted flowering pears, Evergreen Pear and Bradford Pear. The Aristocrat Pear is by far the messiest when it comes to nuisance fruit (See Chapter 6). Once it starts to bear, it is covered with small, marble-sized pears that become mushy and drop off in the fall making a huge mess. For some reason this type of flowering pear is also much more susceptible to mistletoe (See Chapter 4) than the other pears and most other trees. So, if you like trees with baggage, this one's for you. (Fig. 8-9, 8-10)

Robinia 'Purple Robe' — Purple Robe Locust...

"Attack from Below"

The Purple Robe locust was a tree that I once thought was going to fill a niche that needed filling. Instead, it is more likely to fill your property with root suckers. This tree has absolutely fantastic flowers, tolerates heat, wind and drought, has no seeds, and grows fast and not too large. Sounds good eh? The primary issue is that it has a profusion of suckers that pop up anywhere and everywhere from its roots, right through your lawn and the rest of the landscape. There is no easy remedy to this problem that I know of. Every place you cut or nick one of its roots increases the likelihood that a sucker will show up. It has three other problems that also have dampened my appreciation for this tree. If it has too much extra water it gets long vertical splits in its bark. If it is planted in a lawn or in the direct line of sprinkler spray it is likely to get root crown rot and succumbs easily to that disease (See Chapter 2). Finally, if the summer is hot (when isn't it?), it will begin getting yellow leaves and dropping those leaves very early in the season, leaving you with a thin puny looking tree by late summer, when you need the shade the most. (Fig. 8-11, 8-12)

Salix babylonica — Weeping Willow...

"Fast Food for Bugs and Fungus"

Weeping willows are arguably one of the most dramatic and beautiful trees available to plant, but its problems are legion. It is native to areas of high soil moisture availability and high summer humidity. Willows love to grow by ponds, lakes, and streams. The problem

Fig. 8-11: Purple Robe Locust flowers

Fig. 8-12: Purple Robe Locust

is, our valley environment is extremely hostile to this tree. Because its wood is very soft it is like fast food to bugs. It's easy to attack. The stress of living in a hot dry environment also increases its susceptibility to bugs and disease. Weeping willows are nearly always attacked by beetle borers and carpenter worms (See Chapter 4). The leaves are often home for aphids, scale and mites (See Chapter 5). Once the wood is damaged by drought, insects, or human hands, it quickly decays and starts to fall apart (See Chapter 3 — "Wood Decay"). To choose a Weeping Willow is to choose to do battle on a regular basis. It's just too darn much work. For my part I believe trees in my yard are for resting under not continuously working on. (Fig. 8-13)

Sequoia sempervirens — Coastal Redwood...

"An Intolerant Coastal Attitude"

I discussed this tree in the last chapter with my picks, because due to its sheer popularity, I wanted to discuss how it could be utilized. Because sequoias are sure to suffer great discomfort if not damage in our inland environment, and because they require extra attention, I won't plant one on my property, unless of course, I ever have the good luck to own some beach property. Coastal redwoods generally do well, grow fast and look beautiful the first five to ten years after they are planted. The problem is, as time goes by, they are increasingly more likely to fry in the Central Valley, or any valley. They are designed for nearly opposite conditions to what exists in the interior valleys of

Fig. 8-13: Weeping Willows

California. They like fog in the summer, there is none. They like high humidity, there is none. They prefer more acid soil high in organic matter, there is little. They like early cooling in summer evenings, there is none. They like a shady forest environment... look around — it isn't happening here. (See Chapter 6 — "Coastal Redwoods in an Inland Environment") (Fig. 8-14)

Remember, *caveat plantor,* planter beware?

Fig. 8-14: Coastal Redwood

GLOSSARY

Abscise — When a plant cuts off a section of its tissue. Typically a layer is formed that separates one section of tissue from another. The best example is when leaves become detached from a deciduous tree in the fall.

Arboriculture — The study of woody plants and trees.

Aeration — Causing air to circulate through something, such as the soil.

Antitranspirant — A compound applied to leaves to inhibit the loss of moisture through the small pores called stoma.

Auxin — A type of plant hormone that stimulates cell growth.

Cambium — The very thin layer of living, dividing cells that encircle a tree at the outer edge of the wood (xylem) and just under the inner bark (phloem).

Canopy — The leafy top of the tree. The outer leaves and smaller branches of the tree. The whole top of the tree starting from the scaffold branches and working outward.

Carbohydrates — Organic compounds made of carbon, hydrogen, and oxygen, including sugars, starches and celluloses.

Cellulose — The main substance that makes up much of the cell walls of plants.

Certified Arborist — An individual who has studied arboriculture, and taken an exam to show proficiency in arboriculture. The exam is given by the International Society of Arboriculture. Continuing education is a requirement of continued certification as a Certified Arborist. There is an expectation that such certified individuals have a professional level of knowledge about trees and living and working with trees, that includes results from recent research.

Chlorotic — When plant leaves are lacking certain nutrients such as iron or magnesium, they become yellow, sometimes between the veins, and sometimes in the veins. That discoloration is referred to as chlorosis. The plant is referred to as chlorotic.

Co-dominance — When two or more branches grow equally or nearly equal in size and height, side by side.

Compartmentalization — When plants fill tissue with resins and other compounds to section off, or compartmentalize, a part of the plant, usually to protect it from invasion by fungi, bacteria or insects.

Conk — The fruiting body of a decay fungus that lives in trees. A mushroom like structure, sometimes called shelf mushrooms. The conk shows up on the outside of the tree where it creates spores that are spread by the wind to infect more wood.

Copper Fungicide — A compound made in large part out of copper, which is used for killing fungus. It is one of the oldest pest control measures known to man. There are many varieties of copper fungicide available. It is cheap and effective.

Decurrent — This is the overall form of trees that grow in a rounded shape, such as a broad spreading oak tree.

Drip Line — The drip line is the imaginary line on the ground that corresponds with the outer edge of the tree's canopy.

Excurrent — This is the overall form of trees that grow with dominant, strong, upright leaders forming in the center of the tree. They typically have a conical growth habit. It is the "Christmas tree" shape.

Exudate — This is any substance that has exuded, from roots, leaves or other plant parts. It can be the result of normal processes, disease or physical damage, in other words, oozing or weeping.

Fungicide — A compound used to kill fungus.

Fungus/Fungi — A type of plant that grows without chlorophyll, usually with small fine parts. Such things as molds, rusts, wood decay, mushrooms, and mildew are fungi. There are many fungi that cause disease in trees.

Horticulture — The science or art of cultivating fruits, vegetables, flowers, or ornamental plants.

Hyphae — Thread-like parts that make up the mycelium, or body of a fungus.

Imidacloprid — A nicotine-like compound that is used as a systemic insecticide on plants.

Indigenous — Something born, or commonly found in an area. Not exotic.

Instar — The juvenile body forms found in some insects during the stages of growth between egg and adult.

Intracambial — In the cambium area of a tree or other plant. Inside a tree beneath the bark, yet not into the wood.

Larvae — The juvenile body form of many insects between egg and pupae.

Leader — The dominant branch relative to other branches around it of similar size. The longest or tallest branch.

Lignin — An organic substance similar to cellulose, found in woody plant cells.

Microorganism — A minute organism, which requires magnification, such as a microscope, to see.

Mycelium — The spongy mat of thread-like parts (hyphae) of a fungus. The main non-fruiting part of a fungus.

Mycorrhiza — A specific kind of fungus, which typically works in a symbiotic relationship with plant roots to benefit both itself and the plant. There are many mycorrhiza fungi. Some only interact with a particular species of plant, and some are able to adapt to multiple species.

Parasite — An organism that lives in or on an organism of a different species, deriving its nutrition from that host organism.

Pathogen — A disease producing organism.

Pathogenic — Disease producing.

Petiole — The stalk that attaches a leaf to the stem.

Phloem — The bark tissue, particularly the inner bark tissue (vascular tissue) where carbohydrates and other photosynthates are distributed throughout the trees.

Photosynthates — Compounds created by a plant as a result of photosynthesis.

Photosynthesis — The synthesis of organic compounds, especially carbohydrates, from water, carbon dioxide, and inorganic salts, by using the light energy of the sun.

Phototropic — Growing in a certain direction because of the influence of the sun.

Prophylactic — Protective or preventative.

Pupa (pupae is plural) — The usually immobile, non-feeding, stage of growth in an insect's life cycle where it transforms from a juvenile form to an adult form.

Pupate — The process of becoming a pupa.

Refoliate — A word I coined to describe the act of a plant regrowing leaves after they have fallen (defoliated) for an unusual reason.

Rhizosphere — The soil, the area where roots grow. It indicates the complex biological associations that exist in that specific location and that occur nowhere else.

Root Ball — The location where most of the roots are concentrated.

Root Crown — The area of a plant where the top of the roots (the crown) meets the bottom of the trunk of the plant.

Root Flair — The area just below the root crown where the roots visibly flair out into the soil.

Root Zone — The area where you will find the majority of roots from a plant.

Saprophytic — Existing on dead organic matter, such as many fungi, e.g. most mushrooms.

Stoma — The small pore like openings on the surface of leaves.

Systemic — Affecting the entire system of an organism.

Transpire — When plants emit gaseous waste and water through their leaves, usually through the stoma.

Trichoderma — A genus of soil borne fungi that are usually beneficial to plant roots.

Turgidity — The rigidity of plant cells and tissues caused by pressure within against the cell walls by the contents of the cells.

Ubiquitous — Omnipresent. Being everywhere.

Xylem — The interior wood (vascular tissue) of a plant that delivers the water and raw materials from the roots to the canopy and leaves for use.

INDEX

ABOUT THE AUTHOR

John K. Pape has been involved in horticulture since he was in high school. He has always loved watching things grow and is fascinated by the great variety of trees and their complex relationship with human beings.

John has a degree in horticulture, has been a tree climber/trimmer, a landscape designer, installer and maintainer, a grower, nursery manager and owner, and horticultural pest control applicator.

John now is an arborist and horticultural consultant for Providence Horticulture, Inc., which he owns. Providence Horticulture has the divisions of Tree DoctoRx, LandCare Solutions, and Johnny's Garden Nursery. Tree DoctoRx specializes in using the latest techniques and low toxicity methods to help trees stay healthy. Tree DoctoRx treats trees for disease and insect problems and trims trees to highly refined standards. John is on the advisory board for Tree Fresno, and the Clovis Botanical Garden. For the last eight years John has hosted, and continues to host, the "Art Of Gardening," a public television show on KVPT-Fresno, and KCET-Bakersfield.

Contact information for John:
P.O. Box 7735, Fresno, CA 93747
Johnny's Garden Nursery, 6931 E. Belmont Ave., Fresno, CA 93727
Phone: (559) 251-7907 • Fax: (559) 251-5539
Email: jpape@providencehorticulture.com